LIFE IN COLD BLOOD

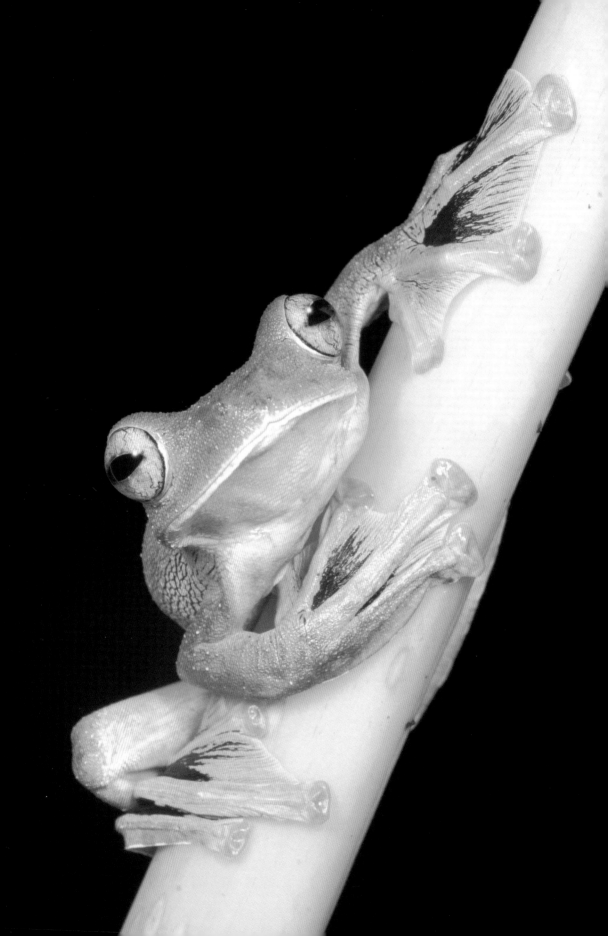

LIFE IN COLD BLOOD

David Attenborough

BBC BOOKS

This book is published to accompany the television series
entitled *Life in Cold Blood*, first broadcast on BBC1 in 2008

Published in 2008 by BBC Books, an imprint of Ebury Publishing,
a Random House Group Company.

The Random House Group Limited Reg. No. 954009

Addresses for companies within the Random House Group can be found
at www.randomhouse.co.uk

A CIP catalogue record for this book is available from the British Library.

1 3 5 7 9 10 8 6 4 2

ISBN 978 0 563 53922 3

Frontispiece: a flying frog at rest

Printed in Great Britain by Butler and Tanner Ltd., Frome.

implacable and predictable rate, exterminating all amphibians in its path. Species that were thriving when the first pages of this book were being written, are now extinct in the wild and seem likely to be lost for ever in the near future. How tragic it would be if the first vertebrate creatures to colonise the land were also the first major group to totally disappear from it.

Reptiles, however, may well be facing a very different future. If the world is warming as many predict, changing patterns of rainfall will cause deserts to spread. Should that happen, reptiles then will be able to extend their ranges world-wide and eventually take over territories in which amphibians and many mammals can no longer survive.

So these two pioneering groups, the amphibians and the reptiles, face very different futures. But that surely makes them both of great fascination, whether we are interested in the past, the present or, indeed, the future of life on earth.

1

Between Water and the Land

Salamanders, newts and frogs

The first forests that clothed the lands of the earth some 375 million years ago were austere, sombre places. The trees that stood ten metres or so (over 30 feet) tall carried not colourful blossoms but pods of spores. No flowers grew on the ground. There, only mosses and liverworts flourished among the rotting leaves that had fallen from above. In those places where rain or ground water were insufficient to sustain such plants, the earth was naked, except perhaps for a few lichens, for there were no grasses. And these forests were largely silent. No trilling songs rang through the branches, no roars and yelps sounded from the undergrowth, for neither birds nor mammals had yet appeared on earth.

Animals, however, there were. Giant millipedes, 2 metres (6 feet) or so long, munched their way through the leaf litter. Scorpions with their poison-loaded tails hoisted above their segmented bodies sought out primitive insects such as silverfish. Of four-limbed backboned animals, however, there was no sign – at least on the land. But in the pools and rivers, swirls in the water indicated the presence of much bigger creatures – fish. And some of them, before long, would venture up on to the land.

When exactly this crucial moment in the history of life took place and which kind of fish was the first to make the move we cannot be sure. The evidence provided by fossils is always, even at its best, very fragmentary. The chances of any individual animal leaving behind fossilised remains are infinitesimal. First, its dead

◁
A young albino axolotl. It will retain its feathery gills into adult life.

9

body has to lie in a place where sediment accumulates. That is most commonly in a lake or the sea. Bones lying on the surface of the land are much more likely to be destroyed than preserved. Next, the sediment has to cover the bones before they disappear, preferably even before they are disarticulated. After that, the mud – and the bones within it – has to be compressed and turned into stone by the great, infinitely slow, movements that distort and crumple the earth's crust. That has to happen without the total obliteration of any sign of the bones. And finally, those bones have to be located in the tiny proportion of rocks which happen to be sufficiently close to the surface for them to be discovered by a prospecting palaeontologist. Thus not only have the vast majority of individual animals disappeared without trace but great numbers of species and families have doubtless existed of which we have no knowledge whatsoever.

It was only in the year 2004 that a fossil was found with all the anatomical characteristics that an animal needed to move from water to land. It was discovered by scientists working in the Canadian Arctic in rocks that had been laid down as sands in the bed of a stream meandering through one of the early forests. They called it *Tiktaalik*, a scientific name based on a word used by the local people for a large freshwater fish that today is frequently seen in the shallows there.

Tiktaalik was a large creature, up to two metres (6 feet) long. Although plainly a fish and covered in scales, it had a more mobile neck than any fish alive today and a huge mouth lined with very effective-looking teeth. But, most interestingly, the bones of its fore-limbs make it clear that it had elbows and that each forelimb ended in a fan of bony rays that could be folded outwards, like the front flippers of a sea-lion. *Tiktaalik*, it seems, was able to use its fore-limbs to support the front half of its body. But that support was probably insufficient to enable it to pull itself completely clear of the water. Maybe it found it profitable to lurk in the shallows along the water's edge and occasionally heave itself up on to the land to search for such invertebrates as could be collected there.

There were other fish living at this far distant time that had

already developed another characteristic needed for any creature that was to spend time out of water – the ability to breathe air. Some were hefty animals, growing up to a metre (3 feet) in length. They too had paired fins with fleshy muscular bases though they lacked the line of bones needed to qualify them as legs. But they did have simple lungs. The evidence for this can, with care, be deduced from some of the better preserved fossils, but we can picture in detail the internal anatomy of these fish because they have living descendants that appear to have survived almost unchanged. They are known as lungfish.

◇

Lungfish have a pair of simple pouches opening from the throat that are lined with blood vessels. So when the fish fills them with air by taking a gulp at the surface, blood passing through their membranous lining is able to absorb oxygen. Three kinds of lungfish are alive today. One *(Protopterus* species*)* is found in tropical Africa and another *(Lepidosiren paradoxa)* in South America. Both these species, thanks to their air-breathing talents, are able to survive in swamps that dry up totally each year. In preparation for this, they dig down into the mud of their evaporating pools, wrap their tails around their heads and encase themselves in a slime that solidifies into a nearly water-tight parchment. Packaged in this way, a foot or so deep in the ground and connected to the surface by a thin air tube, they survive the dry season, breathing by means of their simple lungs. However, in contrast to those of *Tiktaalik*, their paired fins, fore and hind, are slender and whip-like and probably evolved rather later in their evolutionary history.

The third kind, the Queensland lungfish *(Neoceratodus forsteri)*, is rather different. It occurs in three rivers in eastern Australia. Unlike its relatives, it cannot survive complete desiccation but its ability to breathe air by means of a lung enables it to live through the hot Australian summer, even if it has to do so in shallow semi-stagnant pools very poor in dissolved oxygen. It is a big fish, growing to a length of 1.75 metres (nearly 6 feet) and it more closely resembles its fossil ancestors than either of its living relatives. In particular, its paired fins have fleshy muscular bases very like those of the fossil form and from the way it uses them to push itself around in the shallowing pools, it is easy to imagine how valuable they must have been in the ancient swamps.

So the limbs of *Tiktaalik* and the lungs of living lungfish between them enable us to visualise the appearance of the animal, whatever it was, that pioneered the move out of water and on to land. The first creature to spend a significant amount of its life there was a monster about a metre long which has been named *Ichthyostega*, the fossils of which have been found in Greenland. Its snout was so long that its head looks more like that of a crocodile than a cod. It had a massive rib-cage that would have prevented its backbone from sagging when out of water and so allowed it to fill its lungs with air. Its tail, however, was still fish-like and fringed at the end by a fin, above and below. Such a tail looks as though it might well have been something of an impediment on land, so it

is possible that this creature spent most of its life in water, sculling through the oxygen-poor swampy pools, making its way forward with prods of its fore-legs and undulations of its fin-fringed tail. But it might also, occasionally, have filled its simple lungs with air and made its pioneering advances up on to the mud to add insects and other invertebrates to its diet of fish.

◇

One creature alive today can give a faint impression of what those animals must have been like when alive. It is of a comparable size, growing to 1.5 metres (5 feet) in length. Swathed in a baggy black skin, with a paddle-like tail, four stumpy legs and tiny eyes on the sides of its huge head, it lurks beneath boulders in freshwater streams, coming to the surface every six to eight minutes to snatch

13

a breath of air. This is the giant salamander of Japan *(Andrias japonicus)*.

It is entirely aquatic, even though it has functional lungs. In spring the males fight among themselves for the possession of suitable places beneath boulders on the river-bed where they make their nests. Here the females come and each lays several hundred eggs. The male fertilises them and then drives the female away. Then for up to six months he crouches beside the eggs protecting them against predators until at last they hatch. The small creatures that emerge from the eggs are not miniature versions of their parents. Their hind limbs are mere stumps. Most importantly, they lack lungs. Instead each has a pair of fleshy feathery gills through which it absorbs oxygen from the water. It keeps this shape, slowly growing in size, until in its third year it develops internal lungs and loses its gills which simply wither away.

Such an intermediate form between egg and adult that is

△
The biggest of all living amphibians, the Japanese giant salamander. Its size can be judged from the human hand lifting it from the water.

capable of independent life is known as a larva. All insects except the most simple and primitive pass through such a stage of development during their lives and often exploit it by drawing upon two different food sources during the course of their lives, one as a larva and the other as an adult. Amphibians are the only group of backboned animals to have such a stage in their life history. Interestingly, the newly hatched larvae of salamanders are indistinguishable to the naked eye from the hatchlings of the Queensland lungfish.

The length of time different species of salamanders spend in this condition varies considerably. Another species quite similar to the Japanese giant, the mud puppy *(Necturus maculosus)* that lives in North America, does not change into an adult for five years. In Mexico, in Lake Xochimilco, there is another species that may stay as a larva indefinitely and even reproduce in this form. The Aztecs called it 'axolotl' meaning water monster. In the wild, this remarkable creature is dark in colour. However it is so interesting zoologically that it has now been bred in captivity for many years

A young Japanese giant salamander which still retains its fleshy gills.
▽

and today an albino variety is better known than the wild, rarer and fully-pigmented form.

The axolotl is remarkable because it becomes sexually mature while still retaining the external gills of its larval form. It seems, however, that this is due to nutritional problems. The change from larva to adult is triggered by hormones, including thyroxine produced by the thyroid gland. Conditions in this one lake, both chemical and physical, are such that this gland does not develop properly. But that can be corrected. If an axolotl *(Ambystoma mexicanum)* is kept in a tank and a little thyroxine added to its water, the animal loses its external gills, climbs out of water and assumes a terrestrial life.

Another aquatic species, the olm *(Proteus anguineus)*, however, is fixed unalterably in its larval form. It grows to about 30 centimetres (12 inches) in length and lives in cave pools and underground rivers in Italy and eastwards around the Adriatic.

△
An adult axolotl. This is the wild pigmented form.

16

△
The cave-living olm from Italy which, as a consequence of spending its life in darkness, has lost its pigmentation.

Like many creatures that live in permanent darkness, it is blind. Its eyes are physically present, but they are covered by skin. It has also usually lost all its pigmentation and is of an unearthly almost translucent whiteness. Only the plume-like gills on either side of its head have any colour. They are bright pink because of the blood that circulates through them.

◇

Olm, axolotl and giant salamander are all primarily if not entirely aquatic. Other tailed amphibians, however, divide their time between living in and out of water. Newts during half of the year lie curled up in cool damp chambers beneath stones or clambering about in the undergrowth feeding on such slugs, worms and insects as they may encounter. When spring arrives they migrate to ponds in order to breed, usually the ones where they themselves hatched. Now they become truly aquatic. The male great

17

crested newt *(Triturus cristatus)*, soon after he arrives in a pond, develops the finery that makes him one of the most spectacular and dramatic animals of the British countryside, even though he is only about 14 centimetres (5 inches) long. His body is black with a somewhat granular surface, but now, in the water, he develops a jagged crest along his back which continues, with a slightly smoother edge, along his tail. His flanks are spotted with silvery white and an almost iridescent stripe of the same colour runs from his pelvis to the tip of his tail. Most splendid of all, he has a bright orange belly, patterned dramatically with black.

This magnificent creature sits among the water plants, sometimes with a shaft of sunlight illuminating the silver streak on his tail. But he does not start his courtship in earnest until nightfall. Then he moves to an open space among the plants and awaits a female. She is somewhat larger than he is and plumper too, for her abdomen is packed with eggs. He moves alongside her and begins to vibrate his handsome tail. The silver stripe down its side, which reflects ultraviolet light exceptionally well, glints particularly vividly in the dim light of evening. The beats of his tail also create a current that drives pheromones, chemical messages released from his genital pore, towards the female. Occasionally, he waves his tail so vigorously that he may flick the female's head with its tip. Dramatic though this display is, it doesn't always convince the female and frequently, with a beat of her own tail, she will glide away to another part of the pond. But if she is ready to lay, she may well stay.

All amphibians have just a single aperture at the rear end of the body, the cloaca, from which comes both digestive waste and reproductive cells. From this the male now extrudes a small capsule containing sperm which sticks to a leaf or a rock. He moves forward and the female follows him until her own cloaca is directly above the sperm bundle and she then takes it in. Mating is complete.

Within her body, the male's sperm fertilises her eggs. Then she lays them, carefully planting them one at a time on a submerged leaf and folding it with her hind legs so that it forms a neat parcel.

▷

A male great crested newt, in breeding colour. It is only 14 centimetres long but one of the most spectacular inhabitants of European ponds.

Many amphibian eggs are black with the pigment melanin that protects their delicate cells from damage by ultra-violet light, Newt eggs, however, are white and lack this pigment so they need the protection of leaves.

The female produces two or three every twenty four hours between March and mid July until she has laid up to three hundred of them. The larvae, when they hatch, have external gills but they are otherwise very similar to their parents. Almost immediately they start to feed on small crustaceans such as water 'fleas' *(Daphnia)* and other near-microscopic creatures. They feed and grow throughout the summer but by September their external gills have withered and disappeared. They then creep out of the pond and spend the autumn and winter months on land.

Although salamanders are closely related to newts, many of them spend very little of their lives in open water. The European fire salamander *(Salamandra salamandra)* is one such. It is a

△
A female great crested newt delicately wrapping the leaf of a water plant around one of her eggs.

20

magnificent creature, its moist skin a glossy black marked with bold sulphur-yellow blotches. These vary, both in size and distribution. Some individuals seem to have yellow bodies blotched with black. Mating time might be thought to be the one period in their lives when they would return to water, but in fact fire salamanders mate on land. The male chases the female. When at last he catches up with her, he crawls beneath her and entwines his arms with hers so that he is carrying her, piggy-back. He then deposits his sperm bundle on the moist ground and twists his body to one side so that the female is able to pick it up in her cloaca in much the same way as newts do in water.

Her independence from water continues. Instead of laying eggs in a pond which hatch into gill-equipped water-breathing larvae, she retains her eggs within her body. There, nourished by generous packets of yolk that she attached to each one of them, the eggs develop into larvae. The female now searches for open water.

Even a tiny puddle will do. And there she ejects her babies, one at a time. The stage in the larvae's life at which this happens varies. In northern Europe, the newly emerged young have external gills. In the Pyrenees and north Spain, on the other hand, some female salamanders retain their young for so long that the larvae pass through the aquatic phase and shed their external gills while they are still within her so that by the time they emerge they are miniature versions of their parents.

△
The three-lined salamander, one of the large family of North American amphibians that have lost their lungs. They breathe instead entirely through their skins.

◇

The family of salamanders that contains the most species and has the largest populations is found in the north-eastern United States. Paradoxically, these salamanders have lost their lungs, the one characteristic that enabled their ancestors to move on to land. They breathe entirely through their skin, absorbing oxygen in the moist slime covering their skin, from which it is absorbed into their bloodstream. To enable them to do this adequately, the proportions of their body have changed. Some have become greatly elongated with a high surface area compared to their volume. Their flanks also carry vertical grooves which draw up moisture by capillary action from the ground beneath, and so prevent their skin from drying out. The necessity to keep their skins continuously moist in order to breathe means that they cannot wander as widely as the fire salamander or even European newts during the time that they are on land. Many of these lungless salamanders, which belong to the family Plethodontidae, are brilliantly coloured, especially when young – black with pale blue spots, brick red with yellow spots, magenta with black spots. They spend nearly all their time deep in the moist leaf litter of the woodlands so, in spite of their great numbers, they are seldom seen and consequently extremely hard to observe and study.

In one place in Arkansas, however, there is an exceptional opportunity to do so. Some time in the nineteenth century, miners dug a shaft in a wooded hillside in search, according to local

The lungless tree salamander has a particularly long fleshy tail which not only increases the area of its air-breathing skin and acts as a fat store, but is also prehensile.
▽

people, for gold. Why they should have done so in this particular spot is something of a mystery for the rock is a soft loose shale and shows no sign of being gold-bearing. In the event, they did not find any gold and having tunnelled into the hillside for several hundred yards, they abandoned the attempt. A century or so later, however, naturalists discovered that the far end of the shaft had been colonised by one species of this lungless family, the slimy salamander *(Plethodon albagula)*. This, in spite of its unattractive common name (though it is unarguably accurate – their air-breathing skin is exceptionally slimy) is an elegant creature, somewhat larger than a great crested newt, with a black body spotted with white. At least half its length is taken up by a long cylindrical tail. They were there in hundreds. They sat on every ledge of rock, their long muscular tails sometimes clasped around a rocky projection to give themselves security.

The distribution of white spots on their black skin varies. That meant that it was possible to recognise each salamander individually. So scientists started to mark the ledges and take photographs

A female slimy salamander in an Arkansas cave, guarding her eggs.
▽

Newly hatched slimy salamanders have the same body form as their mother and do not pass through a larval stage as many amphibians do.

of their occupants. They discovered to their astonishment that individual salamanders returned to the same ledge, year after year. These small creatures spend spring and summer feeding in the woodlands. At the beginning of this period they court and mate. Then some of the females make their way to the mine shaft and plod laboriously for nearly two hundred yards along it. Eventually each, somehow or other in the pitch blackness, has both the pertinacity and ability to find exactly the same ledge it had occupied six months earlier.

Only the females go to the mine. They lay their gelatinous eggs in clusters, attached to the damp rocks. The young develop into the adult form within the egg membranes. But even though the hatchlings are seemingly far from danger in the darkness of the mineshaft where few predators might search for them, they are not safe – from others of their own kind.

There is nothing to eat in the mine. Most females, during the

25

course of the spring and early summer, are able to collect enough food to build up reserves which they store in their long swollen tails. This enables them to survive the seven months that they spend in the mine, guarding their eggs. But some females fail to do this adequately. You can see which they are, for their tails are noticeably thinner. They clearly have a problem. They solve it, but not by leaving the mine and hunting for more food in the drying leaf litter of the summer woodland. Instead, they eat the eggs and newly emerged young of the other females. They are known as marauders. Whether or not this sort of behaviour happens out in the woodlands has not yet been determined.

◇

One group of amphibians is even harder to observe than the lungless salamanders because most of them are burrowers. You might well come across one when digging in tropical soils, for in some areas they are quite common. As one wriggles through the soil beside your spade, you may mistake it for an earthworm, since many species are about the same size and they all have bodies encircled by numerous rings. But it doesn't move like an earthworm, expanding and contracting its body like a concertina. Instead it has a special way of its own. Its skin is only very loosely connected to the muscles immediately beneath so that its main body can move forward, rather like a rod pushing forward inside a sock, until the skin can stretch no further. Then the skin is hitched up into a new advanced position. If however it is in loose leaf-litter or water then it will wriggle from side to side like a snake. Pick it up and you will then realize that it is not a snake or any other kind of reptile for its skin, instead of being scaly, is soft and slightly slimy. It is an amphibian – a caecilian.

Caecilians may be little known but they are nonetheless both numerous and varied. There are at least 163 species of them belonging to six different families. Many are earthworm-sized but one, from Colombia, reaches a length of 1.6 metres (over 5 feet) and is as big as a python. They are all tunnellers, though a few species live underwater, burrowing in the beds of rivers and ponds.

Surprisingly, since they are seldom exposed to the light of day, one or two are brightly coloured. One species from south-east Asia has a blue-black skin with a bright lemon-yellow stripe along its flanks. They are all carnivores. Of that you will have no doubt if you handle one of the larger species carelessly. It may well suddenly open an alarmingly large mouth, equipped with rows of incurving teeth, and bite you. Its normal diet includes insects such as termites and beetle grubs and especially the earthworms that it so resembles.

The only fossil that can give us any indication of the caecilian's evolutionary history is a highly characteristic vertebra found in Brazilian rocks dating back to some 65 million years. But this one vertebra is rather uninformative and no evidence has yet been found to reveal whether or not this early creature had legs.

Since that time, however, caecilians have become modified in several ways that better suit them to a life spent burrowing underground. They have lost all trace of limbs, not only externally but internally and there is no sign whatever of the bones that must once have connected such limbs to the spine. Their heads, which necessarily have to bear the brunt of tunnelling, have been greatly strengthened, and their typically soft amphibian skin has been reinforced by becoming tightly fused to the bones of the skull. In most species, their eyes are completely covered by skin, for they would in any case be of no use underground. In compensation for the loss of sight, they have developed a unique sense-organ all their own. They have a pair of tiny tentacles, one on either side of the head and each lying in a groove running between the blind eye and the angle of the mouth. These can be engorged with blood so that they project downwards just beyond the edge of the mouth. Each has a nerve supply so there is little doubt that they are sensory organs of some kind. It is probable that they are sensitive to smells and so perhaps help their owners in their subterranean hunts.

The male caecilian, unlike any other amphibian, has what amounts to a penis – a modification of the membranes just within the cloaca that he is able to evert and use to insert his sperm into the female and so fertilise her eggs internally.

Female caecilians, however, have many different ways of dealing with their young. One Brazilian species *(Siphonops annulatus)* feeds them with her own skin. The female lays her eggs in a cluster and then protectively curls her long body around them. After they hatch, the young – at three-day intervals – suddenly and simultaneously start to bite her flanks and tear off strips of skin. She lies there passively, allowing them to swarm all over her until she has been stripped of the entire outer layer of her body. The frenzy lasts for some seven minutes. Then the family rests for three days while the female grows another layer of skin – and another meal.

The female also secretes liquid from her rear end which the young lap up, jostling for the best position to do so. Occasionally she also produces a less viscous liquid which may perhaps contain the pheromone that keeps the family group together in the darkness of the soil or leaf litter.

△
A female Brazilian caecilian with her young which are feeding by nibbling her skin.

In other species, the female retains her eggs within her oviduct for so long that the larvae hatch within her. But nonetheless, she feeds them in a similar fashion. In this case it is not her outer skin but the lining of her oviduct that provides them with their food. They may remain within her, feeding in this strange cannibalistic way, for as long as eleven months.

◇

Caecilians, with their long bodies, may have as many as 250 vertebrae. Salamanders, whose body shape so closely resembles that of the first amphibians, have about a hundred. But the most successful, numerous and widespread of all amphibians alive today, have much shorter backbones. They have a mere nine vertebrae – or even less. And none, as adults, have a true tail. They are the frogs.

There are over five and a half thousand species of them. That number includes animals that are popularly called toads. The name is usually – though not always – applied to those species that spend more of their time on land than in water and in consequence have drier, wartier skins and short hind legs that are more suited to walking than jumping or swimming. The two names make sense in Britain, where there is only one species of truly native water-living frog and only two species of land-living toad. The frogs and toads that happen to live in Britain belong to different families. But when one considers the whole group, worldwide, it is clear that in any single family, there may be some species that have become better adapted to a watery environment and others to a dryer one. So a particular frog may be more closely related to a particular toad than it is to a frog of another family.

To confuse matters a little more, those two European categories are popularly ranked aesthetically. Toads are usually thought of as being uglier than frogs. So when a species, found perhaps in the tropics, was considered particularly ugly it was referred to as a toad. Thus the quite extraordinarily grotesque – but nonetheless wonderfully interesting – species with the scientific name of *Pipa pipa,* is called colloquially the Surinam toad, even though it spends much of its life in water. Such common names have become so well established that it would be perverse and pedantic to try and alter them. Nonetheless, it remains true that it would be more just, less prejudiced – and scientifically just as accurate – to call all tailless amphibians 'frogs'.

But why should they all, at least in their adult form, have lost their tails? It seems that the early members of the group developed a way of getting around that worked as well in water as it did on land – drawing up their hind legs and then simultaneously and energetically pushing them backwards. In water that technique works very well indeed. Humans use it when swimming the breast-stroke. And on land it enables frogs to make truly spectacular jumps.

The biggest of all frogs, the goliath *(Conraua goliath)* from the rain forests of equatorial Africa, which has a body length of up to 35 centimetres (14 inches) and a weight of 3 kilograms (6 lbs 10

The goliath frog is a monster, though the impression of great size given by this individual is perhaps heightened by its nearness to the camera.

ounces) is a relatively poor jumper. Small frogs however can leap extraordinary distances. The champion is a two-inch-long sharp-nosed frog *(Rana oxyrhyncha)* from South Africa which is recorded as having jumped 9.82 metres (32 feet 3 inches) in three consecutive leaps. It may be that a long tail would interfere with the effectiveness of the jumping technique, and a short one would have no function. At any rate, all that is left of a frog's tail is a small stick-like bone, composed of fused diminutive vertebrae, that projects internally from the rear of the pelvic girdle.

These large elongated hind legs have served the frogs very well. The toes are usually linked with a membrane. In water, this opens as the frog kicks backwards and so drives the frog forward. But such a membrane can also be effective in air. The Wallace's 'flying' frog from Borneo *(Rhacophorus nigropalmatus)* exploits the same principle. It has membranes on its hind legs that are even bigger than those of any water-living frog and it lives high in the canopy of forest trees. To move from one branch or tree to another, it leaps forward into the air and splays the toe membranes on all of its four legs. These open and each foot serves as a small parachute, so that the frog's downwards descent through the air is slowed and its forward motion can have its full effect.

◇

The move from water to land triggered another anatomical development. Water transmits sound very effectively. Vibrations striking the flank of a fish are so strong that they pass through the flesh and reach a capsule within the fish's skull that is close to its brain and connected to it by a short nerve. Air does not transmit sound nearly as efficiently as water so such vibrations are fainter on land. Salamanders and newts have a capsule within their skulls rather like that of a fish but nothing more elaborate. So in air the only sounds they are likely to detect are those that are sufficiently loud to create vibrations in the ground that they can detect with their feet. Frogs, however, have developed special equipment to detect these relatively faint aerial vibrations. It is a small circular patch of the skin, held taut like the membrane of a drum by a

▷

Wallace's frog glides from tree to tree in the Borneo forests with the help of particularly large membranes between its toes.

surrounding ring of cartilage and positioned just above the angle of the jaw on either side of the neck. Each is connected to a capsule in the skull by a small rod-like bone. So frogs can hear in air.

They exploit this ability dramatically. The opening between the lung and the throat is partly blocked by an arrangement of cartilaginous flaps and strings that make a noise when air is blown through them. Amphibian lungs are not very powerful so the sound in itself is not very loud. But instead of opening their mouths when they call, as most vertebrate singers do, the frog keeps its mouth shut and amplifies the sound with special resonators. Some species have a single opening on the floor of the mouth that leads to a sac which swells into a large bubble beneath the throat. Others have a pair of membranes beneath the tongue that when inflated bulge out on either side from the angle of the jaws.

In most species, it is only the male frogs that sing. The sounds they make are often described as 'mating' calls. It would be more accurate to call them 'advertisement' calls, for summoning mates is not their only function. They also tell other males of the caller's presence and warn them to keep away. A pond full of calling males in springtime can produce a deafening chorus of sound, audible as much as a mile away. Many different species may be forced to share the same concert hall, for open water can be scarce. The resulting chorus of honks and whistles, squeaks, pings and tinkles may seem initially to our ears to be very confused. But after a little while, you may begin to distinguish a certain vague rhythm.

This is because different species of frogs take their cues from each other. A call may be indecipherable if it coincides with another made by a different species close by. So individuals of one species will carefully and accurately interject their call in the intervals between the notes of the other. It is also the case that different species may not only sing using different parts of the sound spectrum but also have ear membranes that only resonate within their own vocal range, so they are deaf to other calls which may sound equally loud to us.

△
The male golden frog of Panama summons his much larger mate by flashing his brightly coloured hind legs. When she arrives, he jumps on her back ready to fertilise her eggs.

◁
Deep sounds require big resonators.
Above: the tungara frog from Brazil.
Below: the square-marked toad from Tanzania.

Females recognise the call of the males of their own species not only by the particular sound but also by the position from which they come. A call from deep water may mean nothing to them, if they regularly breed in the shallows near the margin of the pond. So an identical sound may be used by two different species.

The little golden frog *(Atelopus ziteki)* of Panama has a particular problem. It breeds not in ponds but beside swiftly flowing rivers. The noise of the water can be so loud that a frog's call would be inaudible. In these circumstances, courting males have to use a different way of attracting the attention of a female. They do so by gesture. They suddenly flick out their golden legs producing a bright flash that catches the eye from a considerable distance away.

A female frog is only attracted by the particular call made by males of her own species. Even so, there may be small differences between individual males. Big ones produce louder songs than do

37

smaller ones and females usually prefer a bigger male as a mate. The females of the painted reed frog *(Hyperolius marmoratus)* assess male vigour by the frequency with which the male emits the notes of his call. Calling however demands a lot of energy and a male can't manage to call continuously with maximum zest. It is only when he detects a female nearby that he accelerates his calls to his top speed.

Having made her selection, she swims or hops closer to a singing male. As soon as she is within range, the male pounces on her and embraces her with his arms either just above her pelvis or just behind her head. Males are so keen to do this that they will sometimes grab another passing male by mistake. The victim, however, immediately complains by making a special grunting release call upon which the grabber will let go. The males become so enthusiastic that they form tightly binding scrums as several struggle to embrace a female. They may even cling with such determination that they eventually drown her.

Sometimes frogs that have apparently been totally absent from

The male painted reed wins a female not so much by the quality of his call but by the frequency with which he makes it.
▽

the land during the dry season suddenly appear in vast numbers after the first rain-storm of the wet season. As a result, competition for females is very intense indeed. It is a phenomenon known as explosive breeding. For all that night the newly refreshed pools are filled with frogs and the air echoes with their deafening chorus. When dawn comes the ponds are brim-full of egg-speckled jelly, but all that can be seen of those who produced it are just a few stragglers returning to their hiding places on land. There can be a similar breeding explosion in colder climates when there is a sudden thaw at the end of winter.

The males of the African hairy frog *(Trichobatrachus robustus)* have evolved a special way of ensuring that they do not miss a mating opportunity because of an inconvenient need to snatch a gulp of air. They grow dense tufts of filaments on their flanks and thighs, their so-called 'hair', which improves their ability to extract dissolved oxygen from the water. As a result they can remain for considerable periods of time underwater, waiting for a female to pass by.

Most males develop special pads on the insides of their thumbs and fingers to give them a firm grip on a female's slippery body. Some are merely warty; others are rather alarmingly spiny. A few grow patches of rough skin on their chest to help them hold their position on a female's back. The male of one largely territorial African species *(Breviceps adspersus)*, who is considerably smaller than the female, secretes a special glue from his skin which is both rain-resistant and insoluble in water and this he uses to stick himself on to a female's back like a small backpack.

◇

After a little time in the grip of a male, a female suddenly and often explosively ejects her eggs. As the male feels them touch the inside of his legs, he releases sperm. In the European common frog *(Rana temporaria)*, small black eggs are fertilised and then the capsule surrounding each begins to swell as it absorbs water and turns into jelly. So a pond fills with huge clusters of spawn and the exhausted females, much reduced in size, hop away.

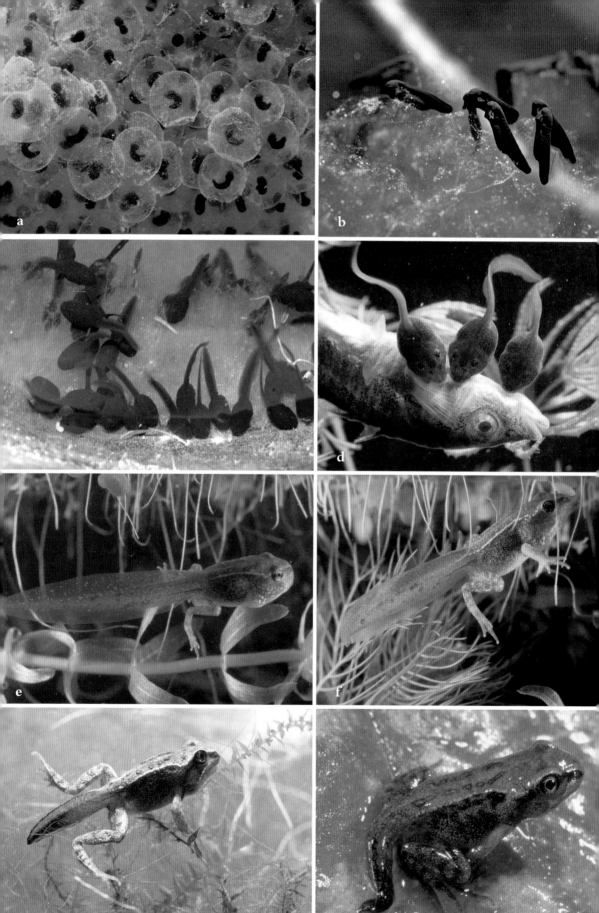

In most species, however, the males will stay in the pond to the very end of the breeding season, in case they get more chances. But eventually they too leave, abandoning their spawn.

Ten to fourteen days later – the warmer the water, the quicker the development will be – the small black dots in the jelly have changed shape, uncurled and gathered together in spaces within the spawn. A few days after that, they become free swimming. Now they have three pairs of external gills on the side of the head – one more pair than a newt larva possesses. And they differ from newts in another way too. Whereas a newt larva looks very much like its parents, these frog larvae look very different. So different in fact that they are given the special name of tadpole. The word comes from two Middle English words – 'tad', a toad, and 'pole' meaning poll or head. Another early English name for these small creatures, 'polywygle', survives here and there as 'pollywog', which means wriggling heads. That perhaps is even more vivid for that indeed is what they are – mobile mouths.

Newts do not take advantage of the opportunity provided by a larval stage of tapping a very different food source from that which will support them as adults. They, right from their first moments are, like their parents, exclusively carnivorous. They start by eating very small animals such as *Daphnia*, and swiftly move on to larger prey, including sometimes younger smaller individuals of their own kind.

Frog tadpoles, however, are different. They obtain their first food by filtration. Within a few days of hatching, a fold of skin grows over their feathery external gills, so enclosing a chamber. Now the tadpole takes in water through its mouth and ejects it through one or more openings in the wall of the gill chamber, passing it over the gills on the way so that oxygen is extracted. That water, however also contains micro-organisms. They become entangled in strings of mucus inside the mouth and from there are moved down into the gut.

As the tadpoles grow, they develop lips to their mouths, each of which carries one or more rows of tiny horny teeth. These enable them to scrape algae from rocks and the surface of leaves. Vegetable matter requires longer digestion than micro-organisms, but by now the tadpole's globular body contains a long coiled gut.

The changes continue. After several weeks, the tadpole, now somewhat bigger than an orange pip and equipped with a quite powerful muscular tail, begins to take an interest in animal matter. Its gut begins to shorten. Two small buds appear on either side of the tail at its base, which in a few days grow into tiny legs. Forelegs are also developing, but those you cannot at first see for they are growing within the gill chamber. Soon however they are large enough to make a small bump on the wall of the gill chamber, spoiling its hitherto smooth streamlining. Internally, the tadpole is developing lungs and some species will begin to breathe air from the surface, particularly if the oxygen content in the water is low.

The eyes, which had started as tiny bulging grains on the front of the head now develop lids which will, in due course, protect them in air. The tail begins to shorten, its substance being absorbed to help fuel the other developments that are taking place in the tadpole's body. Then, eleven to fourteen weeks after it hatched (the precise time depends not only on the species concerned but, within any one species, on the temperature of the water) the little froglet walks gamely out of its pond, still with a stumpy relic of its tail, and prepares to take up life as a carnivore on land.

◇

The ponds in which these developments occur are dangerous places. Snakes and fish, water beetles and dragonfly larvae, even adult amphibians such as newts, will feed on tadpoles and sometimes even swallow the spawn. Predatory birds such as herons also visit the ponds to feast on their occupants. So tadpole losses are heavy. Many frogs compensate for this by producing huge numbers of eggs. A single common European frog *(Rana temporaria)* may lay as many as two thousand. But other species have other strategies to improve the eggs' chances of survival.

Some do so by reducing to a minimum the length of time that their spawn lies defenceless in the bottom of a pond. The female South American bullfrog *(Leptodactylus pentadactylus)* sitting by the margin of a pond excretes a liquid from her cloaca. As it emerges

△
*A dragonfly larva,
one of the many
predators in a pond,
feasts on a tadpole.*

*African tree frogs
assemble on a branch
above open water
and provide a home
for their tadpoles by
excreting a liquid
which they beat into
foam with their legs.*
▷ ▷

she beats it into a sudsy foam. This floats on the surface of the pond and contains the fertilised eggs within it. When the tadpoles develop, they simply drop from the underside and swim away to find hiding places among the leaves of water plants. The female, unusually, remains close by. The tadpoles gather around her and she actively defends them against predators, even attacking the feet of wading birds.

African tree frogs (*Chiromantis* species) also use foam but they produce it sitting on the branch of a tree overhanging a pond. In some species, male and female, clasped together, do so jointly, each beating their feet to make a properly aerated soufflé. In others, males join together and beat their legs co-operatively. The resultant froth hardens on the outside like a meringue with the eggs inside. When the tadpoles are sufficiently developed to be capable of feeding for themselves, the foam liquefies and they fall into the water beneath.

43

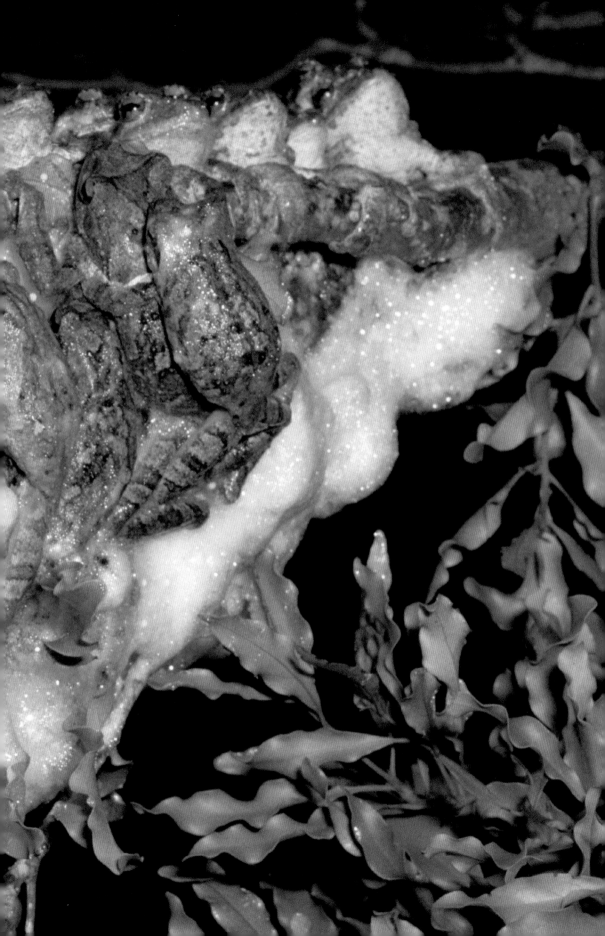

The European midwife toad *(Alytes obstetricans)*, which spends most of its life on land, does not put its eggs in water until the very last minute. The male usually lives in a hole in the ground that is reasonably damp and within a few hundred yards of a pond. When, as a response to his short peeping calls, a female comes to visit him he embraces her firmly with his forelegs. Before long she starts to produce eggs. Several dozen emerge in long strings. As they do, he lets go of the female and crouching on all fours, he releases sperm on her eggs as they lie between her thighs. After about a quarter of an hour, he draws up his legs, one after the other and pushes them into the mass of spawn so that the strings become entangled between them. The action has been described

The male midwife toad protects his vulnerable eggs by carrying them with him wherever he goes.

as being rather like that of a man trying to put on a pair of short trousers without using his hands while lying down. When finally the male frog succeeds, the female leaves.

He keeps the eggs around his thighs for several weeks. If the weather is dry he will ensure that they remain moist by taking them down to a nearby pond and dipping them into the water. The speed at which the eggs develop is greatly influenced by temperature but somehow a male knows when the larvae are ready to emerge. When that time arrives he hobbles off at night to the pond and lowers his hind legs into the water. He will stay there for a couple of hours while all his young wriggle free and swim away. And after all this labour, he may return to his hole to find a second, or even a third female, before the breeding season is over.

The bizarre Surinam toad *(Pipa pipa)* has a body that is so extremely flattened it almost looks as if it has been squashed in a road accident. When a pair comes together to breed they begin a graceful somersaulting dance in the water. As they soar upwards the female extrudes her eggs. The male, grasping her around her waist, expels sperm at the same time so that the eggs are fertilised immediately. The male then extends one of his back legs, with toes splayed so that the membrane between them forms a kind of palette, and with gentle stroking movements, he spreads the eggs over the female's back as though icing a cake. Again and again, the pair repeat their somersault, and each time more eggs are spread over on the female's back. Now the skin there begins to swell so that each egg is soon enclosed within a tiny pit. But still the skin continues to swell and within thirty hours it extends over the top of the eggs. Her back is now once again smooth and unpitted. But beneath it there are a hundred or so developing eggs.

When the young hatch, they continue to develop by absorbing nutriment from their mother's body, taking it in through their infant tails. Before long, the tadpoles within their capsules are so active that the skin on the female's back ripples continuously. Twenty four days after their parents' mating dance, the tadpoles break through their mother's skin and swim off to begin unprotected and independent lives.

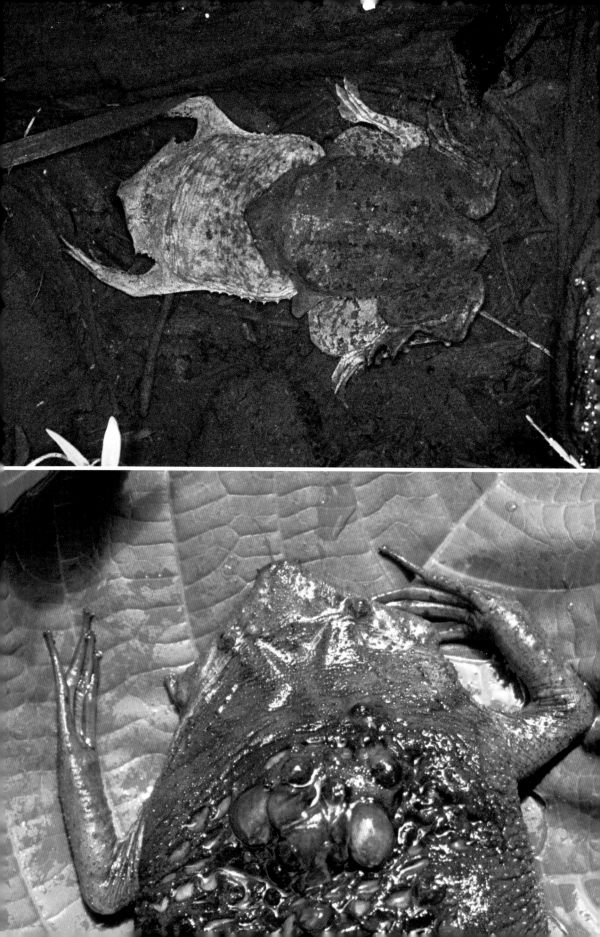

Some frogs avoid communal ponds altogether and use their own exclusive nurseries. The male of one South American tree frog *(Hyla faber)* builds its own private pool just beyond the margin of a larger pond. He constructs circular walls 10 centimetres (4 inches) high enclosing a small puddle 30 centimetres (12 inches) across. Having built his pool, the male sits in it and calls, making a high-pitched metallic clinking sound. When the female arrives, the two mate in his pool. The eggs may be safe from egg-eating fish but there is nonetheless a drawback to the technique. Such a small body of water can easily heat up during the day and so become poor in oxygen. To compensate for this, the tadpoles develop particularly large gills which improve their ability to extract oxygen at low concentrations.

The male gladiator frog *(Hyla rosenbergi)*, who also builds a private pool, deals with the oxygen problem differently. The female lays her eggs on the surface of the pool and there they are held, like a raft, by the surface tension of the water. In this position they can absorb oxygen directly from the air. The problem with this technique is that if the surface tension that supports the eggs is broken, the eggs will sink to the bottom and there die from lack of oxygen. The male gladiator, therefore, guards his pond. He has weapons that enable him to do so – spines like daggers on his thumbs – and he attacks those that challenge him with the particular aggressive energy that gives the species its name.

Both of these pond-builders live in habitats where there is regular and abundant rainfall. The African bullfrog *(Pyxicephalus adspersus)*, however, has to endure long periods – months certainly, sometimes even years – when rain is so infrequent that open water is very scarce. The bullfrogs survive the worst of these hard times by digging themselves burrows and there going into a state of suspended animation, waiting for the good times to return. When at last the rains do arrive, the ponds begin to fill. A sudden heavy storm may cause one to expand beyond its normal margin. Then, as evaporation makes it shrink, puddles are left around its margin. These are what the bullfrogs need. A male will take possession of one and aggressively chase off rivals. On

49

occasion, he even attempts to drive away animals of other kinds, including human beings that he thinks might be trying to displace him. And there sitting in the middle he awaits a female.

Unusually for frogs and toads, African bullfrogs mate during the day. A female visiting him can produce up to four thousand eggs and soon his pool is full of wriggling tadpoles. But evaporation continues to shrink both the pond and the breeding pool. There is now a real danger that his pool will dry completely and then the whole of the brood will be lost. But astonishingly, the male seems to realize exactly what is happening and takes action. Using his powerful hind legs like spades, he begins to excavate a canal to connect his pool to the main pond. Usually this is about 3 metres (10 feet) long but one industrious male was observed digging a canal 18 metres (60 feet) in length. At last the connection is made and the water flows out carrying his brood down into the spacious luxury of the main pond. His tadpoles, now big enough to look after themselves to some degree, have been saved.

◇

Frogs in the South American rainforest have ready-made private pools within easy reach. Up on the branches of the forest trees grow bromeliads – vase-plants – which have a central rosette full of water. There are no fish hungry for amphibian eggs up here and many species of highly coloured tree frogs *(Dendrobates)* lay their eggs in them. But there is little food to be found in such tiny pools and most growing tadpoles have to subsist on algae and insect larvae. In some tree frog species, however, the female has a way of alleviating this shortage of food. She only places one fertile egg to a plant. Soon after the tadpole has hatched, she will return and lay another egg there. But this second egg is infertile. It is no more than a food parcel and the tadpole nibbles at it greedily. Before the tadpole is fully grown, the female may even return with a further ration. In any one breeding season, which lasts about eight weeks, she may rear as many as six youngsters, each in its own nursery and each requiring its tiny mother to make long journeys, up and down tree trunks and along branches, to deliver supplies.

The male of one species, *Dendrobates imitator*, exceptionally, plays a major role in the care of the tadpoles. He may have half a dozen suitable bromeliad ponds in his territory. A visiting female lays her egg, not in one of them but on a moist leaf. The male sits beside it on guard. When it hatches, the tadpole wriggles onto its father's back and he carries it off and deposits it in one of his vacant ponds. But his fatherly attentions by no means end there. He regularly tours his territory, diving into each of his nurseries as if inspecting the condition of his offspring. If a tadpole is hungry, it will nibble his legs and vibrate its body against his. When the female pays her next visit, it is he who decides where she should lay her yolk-rich but infertile egg by leading her with his calls to a particular pond. As she emerges, after having done so, he clambers on to her back and embraces her, clasping her around the neck with his arms, before she leaves once again to feed and generate another food parcel.

A few frogs provide the most intimate kind of nursery. The developing youngsters are kept within the parental body until

A male strawberry arrow-poison frog carries his tadpole up into a tree to deposit it in the tiny pool in the centre of a vase plant.
▽

they have completed their larval stage and have become miniatures of their parents, complete in every detail and faculty except sexuality. The marsupial frog *(Gastrotheca)* does not, as one might assume from its English name, come from Australia but from South America. It does, however, like Australian mammals, have a pouch in which the young develop. In *Gastrotheca's* case, this pouch is on the female. When the pair come together on the ground, the male clambers on to his partner's back and grasps her around the neck. She then straightens up her hind legs, so tilting her body, and starts to expel her eggs one at a time. Each slides down her moist back. As they reach the male, he fertilises them with his sperm and they continue their slide downwards into a slit which runs in a V across the middle of her back. This is the entrance to her brood sac.

One species *(Gastrotheca marsupiata)* lays as many as two hundred eggs. There are so many of them that while they are still at the tadpole stage their mother has to expel them because there is simply not enough room for them all within the pouch. She reaches forward with her hind leg and opens the slit of the brood pouch with her toes. Some of the young then wriggle their way out and make their way into puddles on the forest floor where they finish their development.

Another species however *(Gastrotheca ovifera)* produces only twenty eggs at a time. Each of these eggs is significantly bigger for it has been given a particularly generous ration of yolk. That makes it possible for the tadpoles to stay within the pouch for very much longer so that when at last they emerge into the world they are fully developed and much better able to look after themselves.

Assa darlingtoni, an Australian species, has two pouches, one on each hip. After the spawn has been laid and fertilised, the male stays beside it and regularly checks it for signs of hatching. When he detects that this is happening, he pushes his way into the jelly. The newly emerged tadpoles then wriggle their way through the jelly and force their way into his hip pockets. There they stay and

▷

Above: the male Darwin's frog keeps his tadpoles in his throat sac which, as they develop, swells, sags and frequently ripples.

Below: young Darwin's frogs sit beside their father, assessing their new circumstances.

The skin on the back of a female marsupial frog has split, releasing the froglets.
▽

grow, eventually becoming so large that they bulge into their parent's body cavity, squashing his stomach so much that he is unable to feed.

Other frogs which rear their young within their bodies do not develop special pouches. They use body cavities that normally serve other purposes. Darwin's frog *(Rhinoderma darwini)* lives in the cold damp forests on the southern tip of South America. In this species, it is the male who takes on nursery duties. The female lays her eggs on the moist ground. The male fertilises them and then sits beside them on guard. After a few days, the developing tadpoles begin to move inside the jelly. The male looks at them intently, and then, after a few preliminary swallows suddenly leans forward and takes them into his mouth. He collects the tadpoles belonging to several females in this way, keeping them stored in his throat pouch which is particularly large and extends half way down his belly. There they stay until suddenly he gives a particularly large gaping yawn and the tiny froglets leap out, fully formed.

Another Australian frog *(Rheobatrachus silus)* also seemingly eats its eggs. In this case, however, it is the female that does so and she deals with them in an even more alarming way. They do not stay at the upper end of her body but go straight down into her stomach. There they quickly produce a hormone-like substance which inhibits the production of the hydrochloric acid with which a frog normally digests its food. Not only that, but the hormone also halts the waves of muscular contraction which shift food through the stomach and into the gut. So the eggs remain undigested within their mother's stomach and develop into tadpoles. Her gestatory constipation lasts for about six weeks. The froglets grow so big that her lungs are squashed and she can't use them to breathe. So during the last stages of her gastric pregnancy she has to to rely on her skin for oxygen until at last the fully formed froglets leap out of her mouth. But this procedure may not be without hazard, particularly for the first egg to arrive. Females produce many more eggs in their oviducts than have been found in their stomachs. So perhaps the first few to arrive in their nursery are dissolved before the digestive inhibitor they produce can have

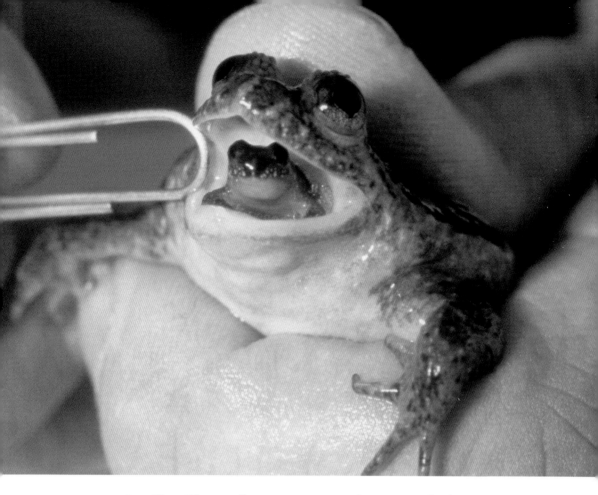

its effect. Very sadly, we may never know any further details, for this extraordinary little frog from one small tract of the Queensland forests can no longer be found and may now be extinct.

△
A young Australian gastric brooding frog, having completed its larval changes in its mother's stomach, prepares to leap from her mouth.

◇

The need to provide a swimming pool of some kind for the tadpoles is not the only factor that ties frogs to water. The character of their skin also does so. The first amphibians to walk on land, such as *Ichthyostega*, seem to have retained the coat of scales that covered the skins of their fishy ancestors. But at some stage, some of their descendants, including those that were to give rise to the frogs of today, supplemented the oxygen collected by their simple lungs by extracting it from the air through their skins. To do that, scales had to be lost and today no amphibian has a scaly coat. A few, however, still carry signs of the scales their ancestors once

59

possessed. *Gastrotheca weinlandii* has a number of plates buried in the skin of its back with spines that rise almost to the surface of the skin. *Ceratophrys*, one of the big South American toads, has a large plate beneath the skin above its backbone. Some caecilians even have scales tucked into pockets within the furrows that separate the encircling rings of their bodies. But all amphibians now breathe though their skins and do so whether in air or in water. For that to happen, those skins must be permeable.

Just as oxygen-bearing moisture can be absorbed through the skin, so liquid from the body can pass through it in the other direction and be lost. Consequently dry air, for a frog, can be lethal. A Venezuelan species of frog, *(Phyllomedusa sauvagei)* lives in an area where there is a prolonged dry season and prepares for it by varnishing itself. Glands in its skin produce a waxy substance and as the dry season approaches, the frog, using sensual movements reminiscent of human sunbathers anointing themselves

△
This frog from the Venezuelan grasslands manages to survive the long dry season by varnishing its permeable skin.

with sun cream, spreads this over its entire body with both hands and feet. One way or another it manages to reach every surface, including the back of its neck and the inner surface of its thighs. Having finished, it shuts its eyes, which were they to remain open would also lose moisture from evaporation. Then, completely coated, it relapses into a state of torpor.

Amphibian skin also contains other glands that produce a defensive poison. The cane toad, *Bufo marinus*, the huge South American species that has spread round the world, has these glands concentrated in patches on either side of the back of its neck. The poison is excreted as a white milky liquid that is so unpleasant to the taste that mammals if they pick up such a toad will immediately drop it. The secretion will also produce a rash on human skin. So effective is this protection that the toad, recklessly introduced into Australia in a misguided belief that it would eradicate the insect pests in the sugar fields, is now a major pest itself which attacks indigenous species of frogs and effectively exterminates them.

In the forests of the Amazon, other tiny frogs *(Dendrobates* and *Phyllobates)* also protect themselves with poison-producing glands. This poison is so effective that the frogs are virtually invulnerable and can therefore develop extremely vivid colours with which to warn off would-be predators and to signal to one another. The poison produced by the kokoi frog *(Phyllobates bicolor)* from Colombia is one of the most potent biological poisons known. The tiniest drop is sufficient to kill a human being. This poison, however, has been the undoing of these frogs. The forest-living Amerindian people catch them, transfix them on a bamboo spit and roast them over a fire. The poison dripping from their skins is then collected and used to make a sticky concentrate with which to tip their arrows – for hunting or for war.

◇

In spite of the permeability of the amphibian skin, a few species of frog have nonetheless succeeded in colonising deserts where there may be no rain or available ground water for months on end.

The brilliantly coloured frogs of the tropical South American forests are all very small, a mere 2 or 3 centimetres long.

Their skins contain a particularly powerful poison used by the forest people in hunting.

Accordingly these frogs, as a group, are known as arrow-poison frogs.
▷ ▷

61

◁ Dendrobates
tinctorius, *Surinam*

▷
Dendrobates
azureus, *Guyana*

◁
Dendrobates
sylvaticus,
*north-western
Ecuador*

▷ Dendrobates
auratus, *Costa Rica*

◁
Dendrobates
pumilo, *Costa Rica*

▷
Dendrobates
leucomelas,
*Venezuela, Guyana
and Colombia*

They manage to do this by absorbing water during the rainy season and storing it both in their bladder and in spaces immediately beneath the skin. Then, bloated with water, they begin to dig. Their techniques vary. Some use their hind legs to push backwards and so go into the ground at an angle. Others, however, use all four legs in a technique known as circular burrowing and simply sink vertically downwards into the ground, swivelling slightly as they go. In either case, the dry desert sand collapses above them, so that eventually they lie in a cavity little bigger than their bodies. There they are well beyond the desiccating effect of sun and wind. But they must nonetheless take special measures to prevent the leakage of moisture from their swollen bodies.

They do this by moulting in a special way. All frogs regularly renew their skin, for being soft and delicate it wears away quite quickly. Many do so as frequently as once a week. The outer layer becomes separated from the new skin growing beneath and eventually splits. This seems to irritate the frog – perhaps it itches – and the frog starts scratching at the loosening skin with one of its forelegs. Somehow or other, it manages to pull a loose edge into its mouth. Then it starts determinedly to champ its jaws, at the same time stuffing the bundled skin into its mouth with its fore-legs and swallowing it until finally the whole skin has been eaten – and so recycled.

Desert-living frogs, such as the Australian water-holding species *(Notaden bennetti)* when they are finally in their underground chambers, do not however eat their skins. They have another use for them. Each old skin remains more or less entire and since it is now separated from the frog's body, it begins to dry out. New layers may be grown every day for a month or more until finally the accumulated skins form a multi-layered parchment-like cocoon, completely encasing the frog's body except for two small holes above the nostrils through which it breathes. The frog will remain within this capsule for the whole of the dry season unless a thirsty Aboriginal, travelling across the desert, detects the signs of the frog's excavation, digs it out and, squeezing it between his hands, forces it to expel its liquid and give him a drink.

△
The water-holding
frog manages to
survive in the deserts
of Australia by
filling up with water
and then burying
itself.

So amphibians manage, one way or another, to survive in places that are far from the standing water from which their distant ancestors came. But their colonisation of such territory is far from complete. Even the Australian water-holding frog can only breed if brief seasonal rains create temporary pools in the desert. Freedom in such areas can only be achieved by animals whose skin is truly and permanently water-tight and whose eggs are enclosed by a shell which can hold the liquid needed for development. And that, indeed, is what descendants of the first amphibians were to eventually acquire.

2

A Return to the Water

Tortoises, terrapins and turtles

We can usually never know in detail the sequence of anatomical changes that lead to a particular adaptation. It is not difficult, however, to imagine those that enabled the descendants of the amphibians to move away from the swamps into the drier parts of the land and to live there, if necessary, without any contact whatsoever with open water.

First, the skin had to be impermeable. Unlike modern amphibians, the first four-footed backboned land-living animals had scaly skins, as did their fish ancestors. So only limited change was necessary to make that watertight.

But complete independence from open water also implies not just living on dry land but breeding there. So eggs had to change. They had to be given a waterproof covering. That also was relatively easily achieved. Special glands developed in the walls of the duct down which the egg passed on its way to the outside world. These secreted a fluid that, before the egg was laid, hardened into either a parchment or a hard shell.

Changes also had to happen within the egg. Amphibian embryos grow by feeding on the yolk provided for them within the egg by their mother. But in the process they excrete waste. In water, that is no problem. The waste in solution passes through the egg membrane and is dispersed into the surrounding water. That, however, cannot happen on land. Instead the embryo, inside its shell, developed a special membranous bag to hold this waste. It is known as the allantois, a name derived from the Greek word for a sausage, for that indeed is its shape. With this device, the reptilian embryo is able to grow within its watertight shell and stow its waste in a container where it is out of harm's way.

A growing embryo, of course, needs to breathe. It requires oxygen. That too was simple enough to obtain in water. The gas in solution was absorbed through the egg membrane. In air, there had to be another way. The allantois provided it. As it fills with waste it necessarily presses tightly against the surrounding shell which is sufficiently porous for gas to pass through it. The embryo's blood vessels which extend into the allantois' membranous wall are able to absorb oxygen from the air and release carbon dioxide. So the young in the egg is able to breathe.

With these changes, backboned animals began to live permanently on dry land. It was, presumably, food that drew them there. Initially, few are likely to have tackled plant material. Cellulose, which makes up the bulk of plant tissues, is very indigestible and animals, vertebrate and invertebrate alike, have to maintain colonies of bacteria in their guts to help them digest it. But there was other food – the long-established populations of invertebrates – millipedes, scorpions, spiders and insects such as ants, crickets and beetles. To deal with such hard-shelled, crunchy meals, the early land-living vertebrates needed strong jaws capable of giving a powerful bite. That necessitated the strengthening of the muscles running from the lower jaw up the side of the skull to the top of the cranium. Bigger muscles required a taller skull. So the flat head, typical of amphibians, changed its proportions and became the more substantial rounded head typical of reptiles.

◇

The major developments of a shelled egg and a watertight skin meant that a vast area of the earth's surface that had hitherto been beyond the reach of backboned animals became available to them. This stimulated an evolutionary spurt and the appearance of a wide range of reptilian forms. Sadly, fossils to show us exactly what these first reptiles were like are even fewer than those that provide evidence about the first moves of vertebrates on to land. This is hardly surprising for the changes from amphibian to reptile, by their very nature, took place on land. There, dead bodies, unlike those in water, are very unlikely indeed to be covered in sediments of any kind before the bones become scattered and ground to dust by the elements.

The changes started in the Upper Carboniferous period about 320 million years ago. The first group of early reptiles that we know in any detail were not unlike salamanders in their general body shape. They had four legs, longish tails, jaws armed with simple spike-like teeth and skins that were either leathery or covered with scales. Their gait and posture, however, began to change over time. Their limbs, instead of projecting sideways, thus giving them the characteristic amphibian sprawl, lengthened and began to change position and point not sideways but downwards. As a result the body was lifted from the ground and ultimately it became possible, for the first time, for a four-legged animal to run.

Two great lineages of these new style creatures emerged. One, known as the synapsids, included forms with odd sail-like crests along their backs. This group was eventually to give rise to the mammals. The second lineage, the diapsids, became very varied indeed. One branch evolved into the dinosaurs and, well before they became extinct some sixty-five million years ago, gave rise to the birds. Another ultimately produced today's lizards and snakes. But two other groups have survived from those very early times essentially unchanged. They are the tortoises and the crocodiles.

The tortoises were the earliest to become identifiable. They were comparatively small creatures and they specialised in defence. In the flesh just beneath their skin, they developed bony plates which enlarged and eventually fused together to form a bony box. The upper part of this is known as the carapace, the lower as the plastron. The scales in their skin also increased in size and reduced in number to form horny plates known as scutes. These lay on top of the bony box, but were separated from it by the thin layer of tissue which generated and enlarged them.

Tracks attributed to one species of them have been found in rocks of Triassic age, around 245 million years old. The first actual bones come from slightly younger deposits laid down about 25 million years later. This animal has been named *Triassochelys*. It was about half a metre (20 inches) long. Its carapace was broad and flat with three rows of large scutes running from front to back and two lines of smaller ones around the margin of its carapace. It had small uneven teeth not only in its jaws but in its palate. Its backbone was fused to the underside of the carapace. So were the bony girdles at the shoulders and hips to which the limbs were attached. Its neck, however, was quite long and could not have been withdrawn into the shell, even if there were room for it, because it carried on its upper surface several pairs of large upward-pointing defensive spines. Its tail also was armoured with rows of sharp spines running down to its tip.

One species alive today can give us a hint of what these early tortoises must have been like – the alligator snapper *(Macroclemys temmincki)*. It is about the same size as *Triassochelys*, and weighs as much as 100 kilos. Like *Triassochelys,* but unlike any other living shelled reptile, it has an extra row of marginal scutes around its carapace. It cannot retract its massive head into its shell. It has rows of stout spines along its tail. And it is ferocious. It does not have teeth as *Triassochelys* had. Instead its hooked jaws have a cutting edge of horn with which it can inflict great damage. Encounter it on land and it is so confident of its strength that it may well attack you. It spends most of its time in water but, in truth, it is not much of a swimmer. Instead it walks stolidly along the bottom of the river and half buries itself in the mud. Then it waits with its jaws open. In the floor of its mouth there is a bright red fleshy filament which wriggles. A fish, attracted by what looks very like a small worm, comes to investigate and with one snap of the snapper's jaws, the fish is swallowed.

Most of the rest of the tortoises alive today are even more effectively protected than *Triassochelys*. They can completely retract their heads into the safety of their shells for their necks are without spines and are one vertebra shorter. Their forelegs are

The most primitive of living turtles, the alligator snapper. The pink filament which it uses to lure fish into its jaws is just visible in the floor of its mouth.
$> \triangleright$

armoured with large heavy scales with bony cores. They too can be withdrawn so that they close in front of the head. Their hind legs can also be pulled in out of harm's way. In some African species, the underside of the shell near the back has a transverse hinge so that the rear section can be raised like the ramp of a roll-on ferry. Another African genus *(Kinixys)* has a similar hinge on the upper part of its shell so that its back half can be lowered shut. All, like the alligator snapper, have entirely lost their teeth. Their jaws, instead, are equipped with blades of horn. Even so, in their essentials they resemble *Triassochelys* so closely that they are clearly members of the same family. In fact tortoises are one of the most ancient kinds of land-living backboned animal alive today.

◇

There are some forty different species of living tortoises. The most familiar, to most people in Europe at any rate, is the Greek tortoise *(Testudo graeca)*. Until recently it was imported in great numbers to be sold as pets. Its name is unfortunate. Linnaeus, the great eighteenth century cataloguer of the natural world, believed that the specimen on which he based his description of the species came from Greece. However, when later zoologists examined it in detail they realized that it must have come from some other part of the Mediterranean coastal lands. It has spurs at the back of its thighs and usually a single plate on its shell above the tail, whereas the tortoises that do live in Greece have two back plates and a spur at the end of the tail. But the rules of scientific nomenclature are strict. A name once given cannot be changed except for some very good reason – and mistaken origin is not one. So the tortoise that is typical of Greece had to be given another name and is now known as *Testudo hermanni*.

Between them, these two very similar species occupy territory all round the Mediterranean. Morning and evening, confident in their armoured shells, they graze out in the open, relishing the heat of the sun. They do, however, have an enemy that can overcome their defences – the bearded vulture or lammergeier. It is a large and powerful bird. Bones form a major part of its diet. To

▷
*Above: forelegs, armoured with heavy bone-backed scales, effectively close the entrance to a tortoise's shell.
Below: the Florida box turtle uses a hinge on the underside of its shell to secure itself.*

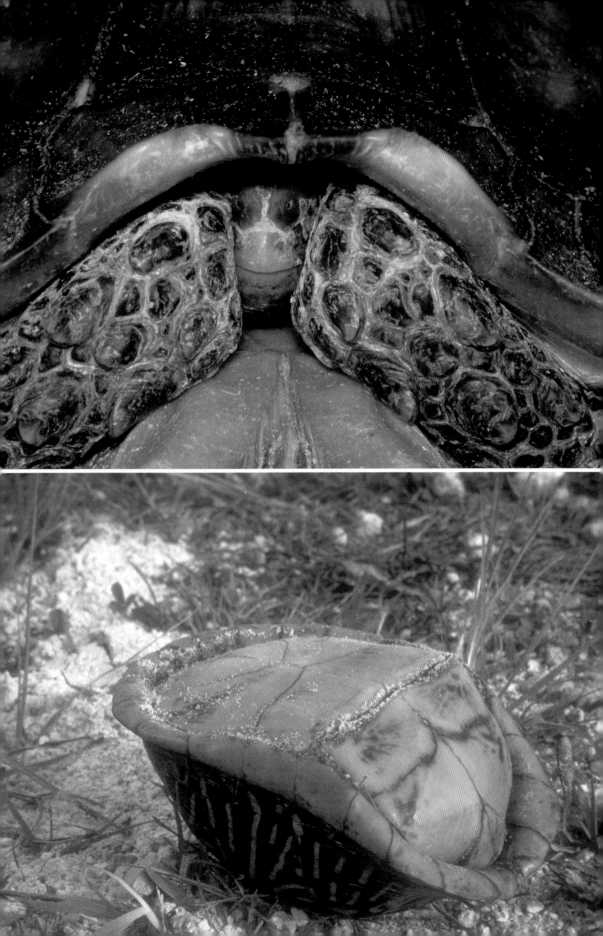

extract the marrow from one, the bird picks it up in its talons, flies to a great height and then drops it, often on a stone that it regularly uses in this way as an anvil. Any bone may need dropping several times before it finally splits and yields its contents. The bird uses the same method for cracking open tortoises.

The most familiar of tortoises, frequently kept as a pet, the Greek tortoise.

◇

In hotter parts of the world tortoises have to defend themselves from the sun's heat, especially during the middle of the day. A body enclosed within a thick shell can easily over-heat. That is a particular danger for the gopher tortoise *(Gopherus polyphemus)* which lives in Florida and other warm parts of south-east North America. It has broad strong claws on its front legs with which it digs so effectively that it can excavate a shaft three metres (10 feet) long in a single day. The work is extremely laborious, for the soil excavated from the far end of the tunnel has to be pushed all the

△
The American gopher tortoise digs tunnels to provide shelter from heat and forest fires.

way back and thrown out from the entrance. A completed burrow may extend for six metres (20 feet) or so. Exceptional ones have been measured that are twice that length. Most descend at a gentle angle and go down until they reach the water table. It is in these refuges that the gopher tortoises shelter during the hottest part of the day.

The tunnel has another very valuable function. At the end of every dry season, many parts of the gopher tortoise's territory are regularly swept by fires. Swiftly moving animals can flee from them or sprint through the advancing flames. The lumbering tortoise, however, is not among them. Caught out in the open, it could be cooked in its own shell. Down at the end of its long tunnel, however, it is safe and an individual may dig several such refuges in its territory so that it is never too far from one in an emergency.

Other animals fully appreciate the value of tortoise burrows.

Foxes, rabbits, rats, raccoons, skunks, owls – all regularly make their homes in the tunnels of the gopher tortoise. So do rattle-snakes, a possibility that anyone investigating gopher tortoise behaviour would do well to remember.

◇

The angulate tortoise of southern Africa *(Chersina angulata),* in common with a number of other species, has a substantial prong of bone projecting from the lower part of its shell just beneath its front entrance. It is particularly long in the males and when they compete for mates, they joust with it. Their technique is to get the prong beneath the front of a rival and then heave and lift. If a male is strong enough, he will manage to raise his rival so high that his front feet no longer reach the ground. Once that is achieved the pusher, who still stands firmly on all four feet, is bound to be able to force back his rival, who stands on only two. So the pusher makes a fast advance. But the effort tires him. With his strength fading, he eventually can no longer keep his rival's

Angulate tortoises fight by over-turning one another. It may take many minutes of leg-waving before the vanquished manages to right itself.
▽

legs in the air. As soon as the pushed has both feet back on the ground, he is once again on equal terms. So the jousting pair trundle first one way and then the other. Decisive victory comes if one manages to make a sideways twist, for then he may be able to flip his rival on to his back. He often follows up his advantage by savagely biting the frantically gyrating legs of the vanquished. Only when the loser lies perfectly still, does the victor leave him to pursue the female over whom they were fighting in the first place. The loser, lying on his back, eventually starts to wave his legs again and will continue to do so until at long last he manages to get some purchase on the ground and can right himself.

◇

Tortoises, with their long scrawny necks and creaking deliberate gait, are often regarded as the very image of old age. And indeed they do live a very long time. The horny scutes on an individual's carapace indicate its age in much the same way as do the rings in the trunk of a tree. They grow more quickly in the warm season than the cold, so each year they acquire a distinct ridge. Counting these ridges therefore can give an indication of a tortoise's age. But as an individual gets older, so the ridges can become worn and blurred and in very old specimens accurate counts are not possible.

A very ancient tortoise lived for many years in the royal palace on the Pacific island of Tonga. He was held in such respect and affection that he was given a name and a title. He was Tui – or Chief – Malila. He had certainly led a long and eventful life. He had been run over by a cart, kicked by a horse and scorched by several fires. His battered dented shell bore the scars to prove it. These disasters seemed to have done him little permanent harm but old age robbed him of his sight and towards the end of his life, he could no longer find his way to the flower-beds where he had browsed so happily and destructively in his earlier years. So every day he was hand-fed with ripe paw-paw and boiled mandioca. Tongan tradition maintained that he had been presented to the then King of Tonga by Captain Cook in either 1773 or 1777. He

eventually died in 1966. If the tradition was correct, and he was reasonably grown when he arrived on the island, he must have lived for around two hundred years and Tonga commemorated him by striking a coin carrying his image.

After his death, however, he was scientifically identified. He was an example of *Geochelone radiata,* a species native to Madagascar. Unfortunately, Captain Cook never visited Madagascar and there is no mention in any of the journals that were kept during Cook's voyages of such a presentation being made in Tonga. So Tui Malila cannot after all be given a place in the record books.

There is, however, another and better authenticated example of a tortoise living to a comparable age. In 1766, the French

△
Tui Malila, the long-lived tortoise reputedly carried to Tonga by Captain Cook.

explorer Chevalier Marion de Fresne collected five tortoises from the Seychelles or Aldabra and took them to the neighbouring island of Mauritius. When in 1810, at the end of the Napoleonic wars, the British captured Mauritius, they also took responsibility for the tortoises. The animals were kept in the barracks of the Royal Artillery in the capital Port Louis. One by one, old age overtook them and they died. The last survivor, like Tui Malila, became blind in its old age and in 1918, it tumbled into a gun emplacement and died from its injuries. If it was indeed the same specimen that de Fresne brought to the island and was adult when de Fresne acquired it, then it too had probably lived for some two hundred years.

◇

Tortoises, like many reptiles, may continue to grow throughout their lives, though the pace at which they do so tends to diminish the older they get and maximum size varies from species to species. Tui Malila, being a Madagascar radiated tortoise, was little more than 40 centimetres (16 inches) long. Marion's tortoise, on the other hand, whose shell is now in London's Natural History Museum, measures 97 centimetres (over 38 inches) for it was a genuine giant. It came from the Seychelles or perhaps Aldabra that lies far away from those islands to the south-west.

Life on a small tropical island is not easy. Nights can be very cold and days bakingly hot. A big reptile deals with this problem more easily than a small one for a big body retains heat better than a small one during the chilly nights and during the day takes longer to heat up to dangerous levels. The supply of food and water on such islands is also a problem, for it is likely to be very irregular. Again a big body can hold reserves built up during periods of plenty which will help it survive barren times. And if there are no mammalian predators on the island, then the clumsiness and lack of speed that is likely to accompany great size need bring no disadvantage. So it is not perhaps surprising that on some islands, tortoises, like some lizards, have become giants.

The Seychelles, from where Marion's tortoise came, lie in the

Indian Ocean off the east coast of Africa. To the south of them lies another group, the Mascarenes – Reunion, Mauritius and Rodriguez. Tortoises reached them, perhaps, by being transported on mats of vegetation that floated down Africa's rivers and were swept out to sea. Doubtless the majority of these involuntary sailors perished in the open ocean, but tortoises can survive for very long periods without food or water. They can also float well for their lungs are at the top of the body so they are self-righting. A lucky few reached land. So every island in both groups acquired their populations of tortoises and there, in isolation and over many generations, they grew into giants.

Alongside them there were other giants – birds. Pigeons of some kind had also reached several of the islands, perhaps blown there during a storm. Once settled, they quickly lost the power of flight. Why take to the air and risk being blown out to sea when there was plenty of food to be found on the ground and no mammalian predators to worry them? With lack of use, their wings atrophied and the birds themselves grew bigger and bigger. Thus Rodriguez acquired its solitaire and Mauritius its dodo.

Europeans first became aware of these giant birds and reptiles at the end of the sixteenth century when explorers rounded the Cape of Good Hope and discovered the sea route to India. The great flightless birds were easily clubbed to death and provided welcome meals for sailors who had had no fresh meat for many weeks. The tortoises too provided good eating. And they had another and particularly desirable characteristic. They could survive on board ships without food or water for months on end and so could be slaughtered to provide fresh meat even after a ship had been at sea for a very long time. So the destruction began.

The dodo was the first to disappear. It set a dismal record for a species. Portuguese sailors discovered Mauritius in 1505 and doubtless became the first human beings to kill a dodo. The last was killed in 1681. For the dodo, there were only 176 years between discovery by mankind and extermination.

The tortoises took only a little longer. There were two species native to Mauritius. They were gone by the middle of the eighteenth century. The two on Rodriguez were exterminated by 1800. That on Reunion disappeared about fifty years later.

But one Indian Ocean species still survives. Indeed, it flourishes. Its home is Aldabra, a remote coral atoll lying nearly eight hundred miles to the south-west of Mahé, the main island in the Seychelles. It is so far from the trade route to India that European ships seldom visited it. Even today few go there. There is no landing strip for aircraft and sailing there from the main islands of the Seychelles takes several days. No one, except a few visiting scientists, lives there.

But there are around a hundred thousand giant tortoises. They live in herds of such density that in places it is hard to pick your way between them and almost easier to walk over them from shell to shell. The island is composed of coral limestone that the rain and the waves have weathered in places to one of the most difficult of terrains – blades of rock as sharp as knives and sink-holes so deep that tortoises which stumble into them cannot clamber out and so starve to death. A significant proportion of the comparatively small island is virtually uninhabitable. The tortoises gather in the few parts where a little vegetation manages to grow between the rocks. In the heat of the day, they seek shade under whatever bushes they can find, even clambering on top of one another to get shelter. Others seek relief by wading into the lagoons of salty mud that accumulates in the hollows.

Plants are so few that one wonders how there could be enough vegetation to support such numbers of animals. But a tortoise's expenditure of energy is very small. And they do not restrict their diet to plants. They will eat anything remotely edible – including the flesh of their recently dead companions. This makes camping there a hazardous business. The tortoises are quite fearless and have no hesitation in bull-dozing their way into a tent to eat paper, slippers, or dirty socks. What is more, they will push aside competitors to reach them. Watching them barging one another in their anxiety to get to whatever is going, you have little difficulty in understanding why on islands, when food is scarce, it pays to be strong, heavy – and big.

Even so it is not certain that isolation was the crucial factor that
led to the tortoises of Galapagos and the Seychelles becoming
giants, for the awkward fact is that the biggest tortoises that ever
existed have been found, fossilised, not on islands but on continents – in India, the United States, Spain and Argentina as well as
on the thousand mile long island of Madagascar.

A camp on Aldabra provides shade not only for human beings but the local giant tortoises.

Tortoises, when they first appeared over two hundred million
years ago, were initially quite small. Perhaps it was the presence
of the dinosaurs that kept them down to size. But when, sixty-five
million years ago the dinosaurs disappeared, the lands of the earth
were suddenly bereft of large animals. The tortoises had their
chance and with little competing with them for food, they
increased in size. Less than five million years ago there were some
that reached 2 metres (6 feet) in length. But their supremacy did
not last long. The mammals, in all their variety and ferocity,

took over and eventually hunted the unwieldy giant tortoises to extinction.

But before that happened, the giants may have spread to islands in the Pacific and the Indian Ocean. Big tortoises can probably survive at sea even better than their smaller relatives. Their shells are proportionately thinner so they have a greater buoyancy and their long necks would help them keep their heads and nostrils above the waves. So it is possible that the ancestors of the giants of the Galapagos and the Seychelles were gigantic even before they reached the islands.

◇

Seychelles giant tortoises are much sought after. Zoos throughout the world used to be keen to have specimens so that they could offer their visitors a ride on a tortoise's back. In the islands themselves it has long been fashionable to keep one as a household pet. It was also once a widespread custom for a newly born girl to be given a young tortoise which she would keep until she married when it would be slaughtered to provide meat for her wedding feast. It occurred to a group of dedicated tortoise enthusiasts in the islands that since giant tortoises could live for two centuries, there was just a chance that somewhere, in a zoo or the compound of a Seychelles household, some ancient tortoises might still survive that belonged to island species long considered extinct.

So searches began. Geriatric specimens that had been living alone for as long as anyone could remember had their shells measured in great detail to determine whether they were something other than the Aldabra species. Some of these venerable survivors certainly appeared to have shells of a sufficiently different shape to suggest that they belong to races that are now extinct. Whether or not the differences are enough to define them as different species is still being debated. Nonetheless, some of these centenarians are being brought together in the hope that, in the twilight of their years, they may find enough energy to revive a species.

On the other side of the world, on the Galapagos Islands in the Pacific Ocean, there are other populations of giant tortoises. They are about the same size as those in the Seychelles and Aldabra and superficially very similar. But they are not closely related for these developed from ancestors that lived not in the great island of Madagascar or in Africa itself but in South America nearly a thousand kilometres (600 miles) to the east. They must, however, have travelled from the continent to the Galapagos in a similar sort of way – swept by currents or rafting on vegetation.

The Galapagos themselves in geological terms are new, having been built by submarine volcanoes erupting on the sea-bed and even the oldest is no more than about three million years old. Some are relatively well-watered. In these the immigrant tortoises found good grazing. Other islands, particularly the newer ones, are covered over great areas with sterile black lava and have very little on them that is edible. In such places the tortoises needed to be able to crane their necks upwards in order to reach the succulent leaves of the few prickly pear trees that managed to take root. These differences in the environment led to differences in the anatomy of the colonising tortoises. Those that fed on grasses on the more fertile islands had a low rounded shape to the front margin of their shells. Those that had to reach upwards for their food developed not only extremely long necks but a peak in the front margin of the shell that enabled the animal to stretch its neck upwards almost vertically. So different islands acquired tortoises with different anatomies.

When Charles Darwin visited the islands in 1835, the official British resident mentioned that he could tell which island a tortoise came from by the shape of its shell. It was this remark that ultimately led Darwin to formulate his theory of natural selection as the driving force of evolution.

The tortoises, however, did not immediately get the credit for this inspiration. It was the practice here, as it was in the Seychelles, for visiting ships to take tortoises away with them and butcher them for fresh meat later in the voyage. Darwin's ship, H.M.S. *Beagle,* was no exception. So Darwin, when he returned to Britain, certainly had specimens of the Galapagos tortoises' carapaces and bones. But, doubtless to his embarrassment, he had not taken

A giant tortoise from one of the more arid of the Galapagos Islands. Its shell is raised to a peak at the front, enabling it to stretch its long neck upwards and browse on branches.
▷

note of the island from which each specimen had been collected. So he could not use them to illustrate his theory. Instead he had to rely on the variations in the size of the beaks of comparatively dull-looking sparrow-like birds, the Galapagos finches, which had been collected by his servant Syms Covington who, unlike his master, had kept careful note of his specimens' provenance.

When human beings first discovered the Galapagos in the middle of the sixteenth century, there were some sixteen different populations of tortoises on the islands. At the time of Darwin's visit there were still a dozen or so in the archipelago as a whole. Today there are only ten, one of which has been reduced to a single individual known sadly as Lonesome George, who lives in his solitary old age in the scientific research station on one of the islands.

The biggest surviving population inhabits the grassy slopes around the rim of the crater of Alcedo, the great volcano on Isabela Island. There the animals perambulate slowly around grazing the short turf. In between meals, they sit almost motionless, placidly gazing at the world around them. If you approach them they show little fear. Only when you are really close by do they bother to withdraw their heads into their shells with a hiss.

Their necks are proportionately much longer than, for example, that of the familiar 'Greek' tortoise and the opening of the shell into which they withdraw them is comparatively wide so that even with their fore-legs closed in front of them, enough of their flesh is exposed for a predator like a dog or a cat to be able to bite it. But there are none such here, so this does not create a problem. Indeed, the tortoises seem quite oblivious of any such danger. When they sleep, they do so with their necks still extended and resting on the ground in front of them. In the security of the predator-free Galapagos the shells are no longer needed for defence. Which is just as well, for they no longer provide it. Nonetheless, shells bring real inconveniences. For one thing, they make it impossible for an individual to rid itself of any ticks or other skin parasites that might attach themselves. To do that a tortoise has to recruit helpers. In the Galapagos, mocking birds,

In the absence of any aggressive predators on its island, a giant Galapagos tortoise is able to sleep safely with its long neck exposed.
◁

abundant on the islands, tackle the job with enthusiasm. To summon them, a tortoise stiffens its legs and raises its heavy shell off the ground. The posture is unambiguous and obvious and usually within seconds one or more mockingbirds have appeared and are hopping busily over the dry wrinkled folds of the tortoise's neck and right up its legs to probe deep into the cavity of its shell.

The North American wood tortoise *(Chelonoides carbonaria),* has a different solution to the problem of toiletry. It recruits ants to rid it of its parasites. It simply walks into an ants' nest and sits there while the insects swarm all over it, penetrating deep inside its shell, picking off any parasites they might find.

◇

A shell also makes copulation difficult. Mating in a suit of armour can hardly be expected to be easy. However, the male tortoise, unlike any male amphibian, does have a penis, an organ arising

△
A giant tortoise cannot scratch its skin to remove ticks or other parasites. So it relies on ground finches and other birds to do so and signals that it is requiring such help by standing stiff-legged.

▷
Giant Galapagos tortoises spend a great deal of time in copulation.

internally from the lower wall of the cloaca which, when erect, projects backwards below the tail.

A female tortoise who is ready to mate leaves a strongly smelling trail along the ground from her cloaca. A male, on coming across this, will follow the trail, if necessary for some hours until at last he catches up with her. He then uses his great forelegs to heave himself up on to her shell. Ideally he does this from the rear so that he will be conveniently placed to bring his penis forward and insert it into her genital tract.

Sometimes in his enthusiasm to reach a female before his competitors his approach is more lateral. However, he has a neat method of putting this right. The underside of his shell carries a shallow longitudinal groove down the centre. If he approaches a female from the rear, then this groove fits neatly over a ridge that runs along her back above her backbone. But when he comes at her from the side, the groove on his underside crosses her ridge at an angle. In that case, as he teeters precariously on top of her shell, he gives himself a sideways push with one of his pillar-like hind legs so that he slowly swivels until, with a thud, his furrow slots onto her ridge and he is ready for action.

◇

A shell brings yet another inconvenience. It is a heavy load to have to carry about at all times. There is one way to alleviate that – by going for a swim. And where there is water there is often also food – lush vegetation, insect larvae, amphibians, even fish. So it is hardly surprising that large tortoises living near rivers, streams and ponds regularly visit them.

In the African forest the biggest of the hinged tortoises, *Kinixys homeana*, regularly swims and feeds in water. The Burmese brown tortoise *(Manouria emys)* is even bigger with a shell that can measure up to 60 centimetres (2 feet) long. The female, uniquely among tortoises, uses her great weight and commensurate strength to defend her nest and eggs and aggressively head-butts those that get too close. But it too spends a considerable amount of time taking the weight off its feet by lounging in forest pools.

An adult red-eared terrapin, some 20 centimetres long, whose tiny hatchlings are frequently kept in domestic aquariums.

Most terrapins, like these red-eared in Texas, spend much of their time out of water. But suitable safe basking sites often become very crowded.
▷ ▷

Smaller species also respond to the rewards that water can provide. The Emydidae, known more colloquially as the emydids, are pre-eminent among those that have done so. There are 85 different species of them and they are found throughout the northern and subtropical areas of Africa, Eurasia and North America. A few pay only fleeting visits to open water but most of them spend a great deal of their lives swimming.

The local North American people, the Algonquin, called these little creatures 'torapé'. The first European settlers adopted the name, anglicised it as 'terrapin' and eventually used it much more widely.

This perhaps is the place to mention the confusion that exists in the names used for reptiles with shells. In North America, all of them are spoken of as turtles. In the English used in Europe, however, they are given different names according to their habitat. Those that are mostly or entirely land-living are called tortoises.

Those that divide their time between land and water are usually termed terrapins and those that spend their lives almost entirely in water are known as turtles. That is the way the different names will be used here.

The terrapins that the Algonquins called torapés are the small creatures that today are often kept as pets. They are usually sold when they are scarcely more than hatchlings a few inches long. In spite of the fact that they are often put in aquaria, they really require places where they can emerge from the water to bask. As youngsters, some species are pretty, dainty creatures. One of the most commonly kept is the red-eared terrapin *(Trachemys scripta elegans)* which is bred commercially. It has a green and yellow head with a red stripe running from behind its eye which it engagingly exposes every time it extends its neck. These little terrapins, however, grow. They can reach a length of 20 centimetres (8 inches), and become too big for the space available for them in their owner's home. Many zoos are offered far more adult specimens than they can accommodate. Others are released into the wild. In the northern parts of Europe, they can only survive the winter with difficulty but the climate of the Mediterranean suits them quite well and there permanent breeding populations have become well established.

Most terrapins in the wild are found in North America, although they do extend across Eurasia and live in lands both to the north and the south of the Mediterranean. One, the pond terrapin *(Emys orbicularis)* ranges as far north as Latvia and the southern Baltic. The largest of them all is an Indian species, *Megachelys trijuga,* which grows to nearly 60 centimetres (2 feet) but most of them are much smaller. Between them they range from being totally land-living to almost entirely aquatic with all stages of amphibious life in between. The terrestrial species have stumpy club-like legs. Those that are more aquatic have developed fringes of skin between their toes, and swim by kicking backwards with their hind legs.

The ability to withdraw the head into the protection of the shell was acquired by tortoises and terrapins surprisingly late in their evolutionary history. Tortoises and emydids do so by bending their necks vertically into the shape of an S. One group of terrapins, however, evolved a different way of retracting their heads. They bend their neck horizontally. This in practice allows the neck to be much longer. Though both groups have the same number of neck vertebrae – eight – those that bend their necks laterally are able to develop very long necks indeed and the snake-necked turtles of South America and Australia have taken full advantage of the possibility. Their necks, together with their heads, are even longer than the length of their shells. Picking up one of these has to be done with the greatest care. If you grip it by its shell you are likely to get bitten. The only safe way to hold it is by its hind legs.

The most bizarre of these side-necked turtles is the South American mata-mata *(Chelys fimbriata)* It is a big creature with a shell that alone measures some 40 centimetres (16 inches). Its head, long neck and legs are hung around with ragged tatters of skin that obscure its outline very effectively indeed. Algae usually grow over its rough corrugated shell and it habitually lies on the bottom of ponds where

The South American mata-mata turtle is so well disguised that prey often wander close to it and are suddenly snapped up.
▽

it is virtually invisible. Its jaws are degenerate, little more than toothless rods that extend back almost to its ears. But if tadpoles or small fish swim into range it suddenly straightens the bend in its neck so that its head shoots forward. At the same time it gapes, creating a suction that sweeps its prey into its mouth.

◇

The advances that enabled the ancient reptiles to colonise the dry lands of the earth became liabilities to those of their descendants who returned to water. The scaly watertight skin certainly prevented tortoises from drying out in deserts but it prevented their descendants, the turtles, from breathing through their skins when in water as their even more distant amphibian ancestors had done. So most terrapins and turtles have to return regularly to the surface to gulp air. One family of turtles, however, has developed a way of reversing this change. The soft-shelled turtles have lost all horny scutes on their shells. In their place, the bones of their carapace are covered with a leathery skin which carries blood vessels within it, close to the surface. This enables the animals to absorb oxygen from the water in much the same way as newts and frogs do.

These soft-shelled turtles are very successful. There are twenty-two species of them living in the warmer parts of all the continents except Australia and South America. One of them, the giant Malaysian soft-shell *(Pelochelys bibroni)*, grows to a length of up to a metre (3 feet) and will even venture into estuaries and occasionally goes some way out to sea.

The other major advance that enabled reptiles to colonise the land, the shelled egg, also became a major limitation to those that returned to water. The embryos within such eggs breathe air through their allantois and will drown if they are put in water. So a terrapin or a turtle, even though it spends virtually all its time in water and finds all its food there, has to return to land to nest.

The level and extent of fresh waters may vary extremely. The pig-nose turtle *(Carettochelys insculpta)* lives in New Guinea and a few parts of northern Australia. Here rivers flow between high

△
The short proboscis of the pig-nose turtle enables it to breathe air with only a minimum of its soft shell above water.

banks and may rise and fall many metres. At the end of the dry season, when the rivers are at their lowest, the female pig-nose climbs up the river bank and digs a hole close to the top in which she lays twenty or so large spherical hard-shelled eggs. It takes seventy days for the embryos within the eggs to develop to the point where they are fully formed. But if the rains are late, the river will be reduced to a chain of shallow pools far below the level of the nest. If the young turtles were to emerge at such a time they would easily be caught by birds and other predators even if they managed to get as far as the pools. But the eggs do not hatch. They wait safe in the sand. When the rains at last arrive, the waters rise and reach the nest. The young, waiting within their shells, detect that this has happened by the rapid drop of oxygen reaching them through the gas-permeable shell. Within seconds, the young pig-noses burst explosively from their shells and swim away in the newly-arrived river waters.

In the Amazon basin, freshwater turtles face a rather different problem. Here every year, the rivers rise and flood land for up to twenty-five miles on either side. The arrau *(Podocnemis unifilis),* one of the largest of freshwater turtles growing up to a metre (3 feet) long, ranges widely during the rainy season feeding on fallen fruit in the flooded forest.

But when the waters begin to fall, the arrau start to travel to their breeding grounds. They seem to know which shoals in the swollen river will eventually become exposed and will travel as much as a hundred miles in order to reach such places. As the river continues to fall they assemble in thousands. Smaller waterways become so blocked by their packed bodies that the noise of their shells clinking together can be heard from considerable distances. As the water continues to fall and the sandy shoal begins to dry out, so the hordes of turtles climb out of the water and start to dig holes for their eggs.

The sandbank may not be exposed for long so the turtles have no time to waste. As each female lays and leaves so others take her place, often digging in the same patch of sand and destroying the eggs of their predecessors. Each female will produce about eighty eggs, burying them high on the banks beyond the immediate reach of the river water. But she has a unique technique of ensuring that her eggs hatch before the waters return and drown them. She retains them in her oviduct even after they have started to develop and while she is still swimming awaiting the drying out of her nesting grounds. If she can, she spends time basking on logs, warming her body so that the development of her eggs will be speeded. As a result her eggs, once they have been laid, have the shortest development period of any turtle – 45 days, about half the time taken by those of most turtles.

◇

The similarity between terrapins and tortoises make it clear that they are closely related and it may well be that today's terrestrial torrtoises had an aquatic parent. The earliest fossil terrapins come from the Oligocene, and are around 30 million years old. But the

△
The arrau, or freshwater turtle of the Amazon, lays its eggs in holes which it digs in the river's sand banks.

first shelled reptiles to return to the water made their move long before that. Some did so 150 million years ago in the Upper Jurassic. These were the first marine turtles.

Their earliest fossils so far discovered are already well adapted to an aquatic life. Their hind legs have become broad and fin-like and their forelimbs have changed from pillar-like legs able to lift and transport a heavy body across the ground into long, graceful and powerful oars. By Cretaceous times, a hundred million years ago, a great number of different species of them were cruising the seas, among them a giant, *Archelon,* the biggest turtle that has ever existed with a carapace three metres (10 feet) long and an even greater width, if measured with its huge paddles outstretched. Its bony carapace has been reduced from a continuous shield to a line of bones around its margin which are supported by thin flat struts extending at right angles from the spine. This reduction of bone presumably brought them a loss of weight and a valuable increase in buoyancy.

Today's turtles show a further progression in these processes of adaptation to life in water. Their carapaces have been made even lighter by reducing the extent of the internal bony shield so that the ribs project beyond its margin on either side. Their hind legs are still relatively short but they are webbed and used as rudders, since turtles propel themselves through the water entirely by strokes of their long front flippers – a much more efficient way of swimming than the hind leg kicks of the terrapins.

Today there are seven surviving species of marine turtle. The smallest of them, the ridley turtles, are only about 60 centimetres (2 feet) long. There are two closely related species, one on either side of the Isthmus of Panama. That distribution is not as odd as today's map might make it seem, for over the past few million years the isthmus has been underwater several times, so doubtless both species are descended from one common stock. The Atlantic ridley *(Lepidochelys kempi)* is largely restricted to the Caribbean and the Bay of Mexico though wanderers sometimes turn up along the eastern coast of North America. The Pacific ridley *(Lepidochelys oliveacea)*, on the other side of the isthmus, is much more widely distributed and ranges from the western coast of the United States all across the Pacific even as far as India.

The hawksbill *(Eretmochelys imbricata)* is rather larger and distinguished by the fact that the horny scutes on its back overlap one another like tiles on a roof. These scutes provide the material that is used ornamentally and is known – just to confuse nomenclature still further – not as turtleshell (which it is) but tortoiseshell (which it is not, whether one speaks as a North American or a European).

The loggerhead *(Caretta caretta)* has a particularly broad head which carries powerful jaw muscles. These enable it to bite through not only the shells of molluscs but even coral. It can be found in reefs throughout the tropical oceans and has even colonised the Mediterranean.

The commonest and best known of all is the green turtle *(Chelonia mydas)* which is also found in reefs world-wide. A very similar closely related species, the flatback *(Chelonia depressa)*, is restricted to the coastal seas of northern Australia.

△
A hawksbill turtle, easily recognised by the jagged edges of its shell.

These six are, in their essentials, all very similar. But there is one, the biggest of all, that differs so much from the others that it is allocated to a family of its own. This is the leatherback *(Dermatochelys coriacea)*. It is a colossus, nearly two metres long (6 feet) and weighing up to half a tonne. It, of all living turtles, is the most extremely adapted to an ocean-going life. It has taken the reduction of the carapace to the extreme. It has lost it altogether. When it is immature, the young leatherback develops an extraordinary mosaic of tiny bony platelets in its skin but as it grows even these are absorbed and lost. All that survives in the adult animal is a small butterfly-shaped plate at the back of the neck which articulates with one of the vertebrae. The horny scutes have also gone and the animal's huge back is covered with a smooth oily skin which is raised into five long shallow ridges running its length.

◇

Turtles, like giant tortoises, find it difficult to rid themselves of skin parasites and regularly visit cleaning stations where fish do this for them – and thus get a meal for themselves.

These seven species between them range throughout the tropical seas and sometimes wander into northern European waters. Swimming reduces some of the problems that a heavy cumbersome shell brings to a land-living tortoise. Weight is much less of a handicap to an animal that spends its life supported by water. Even ridding itself of parasites is easier, for the seas of the world are full of fish eager and willing to make a meal of the worms, lice, algae and other organisms that only too readily attach themselves to a turtle's shell. So there are cleaning stations on coral reefs where turtles make regular calls to be tended by fish that station themselves there to provide a cleaning service.

But there is one major disadvantage to their way of life that turtles have never overcome. They, like all reptiles, must still lay their eggs on land. The entire world population of Atlantic ridleys do so on remote beaches in north-eastern Mexico. These beaches, however, are on the coast of the mainland and that means that they are accessible to a multitude of egg-eaters – raccoons, coatis, feral pigs and dogs as well as birds such as vultures, ghost crabs and those ubiquitous predators, human beings. The ridleys' solution to these threats is dramatic in the extreme. They overwhelm the egg-eaters by sheer numbers.

The adult turtles assemble in the shallow seas just off the coast. Then one morning, when the tide is high, they start their arrival, their *arribada*. They clamber out of the lapping waves in thousands. The beach becomes black with them as they start digging holes in which to deposit their eggs. The predators steal the eggs almost as soon as they are laid, but still the turtles come. Before long, the egg-eaters can eat no more, so those eggs that were laid last stand a better chance of survival. The procession from the sea continues until evening. Then suddenly the ridleys vanish. The adults will not be seen again for another year.

◇

Sunset on a beach in north-eastern Mexico. Atlantic ridley turtles come ashore for their annual mass egg-laying.
▷▷

Some leatherback turtles also lay their eggs on mainland beaches but most of them choose remote islands where predators are much fewer. They also lay not during the day, as the ridleys do,

but at night under cover of darkness. The journey from sea to land for such big creatures is hard and laborious. A female needs to reach the head of the beach for only there will her eggs be safe from being soaked and drowned during their development by high tides. One night, soon after sunset, she swims into the shallows and starts the long haul up the beach. She is not alone. There are other black domes every few yards along the length of the beach.

It is exhausting work. She hauls herself forward with her front flippers, moving them together in a terrestrial version of the breast-stroke. They do not lift her shell but drag it along the sand. Every few yards, she presses her flippers downwards to take some of the great weight of her body and allow her to fill her lungs with air. Her eyes, when underwater, are lubricated by a special mucus from her tear glands, but now, out of water, this trickles down her cheeks and becomes clogged with sand so that she appears to be weeping.

△
A leatherback, the biggest and most wide-ranging of living turtles, attended by a shoal of remora fish, some of which have fastened themselves to its shell.

At the head of the beach the sand is drier and each stroke of her flippers throws it into the air. She may turn to the side once or twice so that her trail up the wave-smoothed part of the beach will not lead directly to her laying place.

She begins to dig, hurling the sand in the air. Within five minutes she has excavated a wide pit for herself. But she is unlikely to be the first here. A sweep from her flipper may expose the eggs of others that preceded her, but they are disregarded and flung backwards.

Half a metre (20 inches) down, and the sand is firm and moist. Using her surprisingly mobile hind legs alternately, she carefully digs a small shaft. She pauses and then begins to deposit her eggs into the shaft using one of her hind flippers, delicately curved to guide them down to the bottom of the hole and break their fall. They emerge from her cloaca, mostly one at a time but sometimes in groups of three or four, until she has produced a clutch of up to a hundred or so. It takes her about half an hour.

Carefully, she trowels sand back into the egg shaft with

A female leatherback turtle starts digging her nest hole, flinging sand over herself with swipes of her front flippers.
▽

delicate, accurate and alternate strokes of her hind legs and then fills in the whole pit with swipes of her front flippers. She brushes the surface with dry sand, swivels her huge body and moves away to one side. It seems for a minute or so that she is starting to dig another pit. But she doesn't persevere. Whether she intends it or not, her tracks now give a false idea of where she actually deposited her eggs. And then, at last, she swivels one last time, faces down the beach and heads for the sea.

But once in the water, she doesn't swim far. She may remain a short distance off shore for another few weeks, producing more eggs and accumulating them in her oviducts. Then she pays another visit under cover of darkness to the nesting beach. She may lay as many as six clutches in one season before she finally leaves the off-shore waters. The effort has been huge and she will not repeat it the following year. It may, in fact, be as long as eight years before she sets off once again on the long voyage to the nesting grounds. But when she does, it will be to this very same patch on the very same beach.

◇

The length of time turtle eggs take to hatch depends to some degree on the temperature of the sand. If they have been laid in a place that is regularly warmed by the sun, they may do so in fifty days. Other clutches in other sites may take as long as seventy. When they are fully developed, the young in the eggs deep in the sand slit the parchment shell that encloses each of them with a tiny spike on the tip of the nose.

As each struggles from its shell, it starts to make a little space for itself. It digs away at the sand above it which falls down and is compacted with its feet. Soon the increasing number of hatchlings have created a little subterranean chamber that slowly rises upwards. Finally, one night, one of the youngsters breaks through the surface. Then all of them erupt and pour out in a stream across the sand. Frantically flailing their flippers, they race down towards the water.

The cue that guides them to the sea is not the slope of the

◁
The broad hind flippers of a female leatherback gently steer her eggs into the shaft she has dug for them.

beach, nor even the sound of the waves, but the light in the sky which is brighter above the sea than above the land, whatever the weather. If they emerged during daylight hours, the majority of them will be pounced on by vultures and gulls and swallowed alive. At night they have a better chance. But when they reach the water, the dangers increase, night or day, for there predatory fish have assembled to await them. As soon as the tiny hatchlings reach the wavelets swilling up the shore and are swept away by them they instinctively swim down to the sea floor so that they are carried out to sea by the undertow as quickly as possible.

For a short time, the yolk that remains in their infant stomachs sustains them. Thereafter, perforce, they will starve until they reach the comparative safety of the open ocean. There, they feed on the tiny plants and animals that constitute the floating meadows of the sea, the plankton, as they are swept along by the currents. Those that survive eventually become big enough and

△
Newly emerged hatchlings of a green turtle start their run for the sea.

strong enough to take their own course through the water and seek out their own feeding grounds, very often close to the floor of the shallow coastal seas.

Only a tiny proportion of those that hatched reach maturity. Of these, some are ready to breed by the time they are eight years old. Others may not reach that point for several decades. But eventually, they all become possessed by the urge to breed.

Now starts a stage in their lives which is still a mystery to us. Fully grown, turtles are such powerful swimmers that they are able to determine in which direction to travel, irrespective of ocean currents. No matter how far they have wandered during their juvenile years, they start to journey back to the beaches where they were hatched.

The distances involved may be immense. A high proportion of the green turtles in the Atlantic hatched on the beaches of the remote island of Ascension. Many of these will have been carried by the currents towards the east coast of Brazil where they have been feeding for several years. But when breeding time comes, they start to make their way back. It is a journey of around 2,500 kilometres (1,500 miles). Ascension Island is only 11 kilometres (7 miles) across.

Reaching it across such an immense distance is an extraordinary navigational feat. It is thought that turtles steer by the sun and that they are also able to sense the earth's magnetic field. How they recognise that they have, in fact, arrived is also a mystery. Perhaps some faint smell of their natal beach lingers in their memory and acts as a guide. The fact remains, however, as attested by a great number of tagging programmes, that the turtles seeking to breed return to the beach of their birth.

The males cruise offshore, waiting for the females. They quarrel and fight among themselves as they strive to couple with an arriving female. The successful suitor bites her shell and then clasps her over her shoulders with his flippers. The load on her is huge. She needs to return to the surface in order to breathe, but her efforts to do so only too often result in the male on her back breaking the surface and filling his lungs while she is still left

below water struggling to get a breath.

Copulation may last for six hours, but eventually the male breaks away and resumes his patrols, looking for another mate. She remains sexually attractive for a whole week and she may mate several times more, building up a store of sperm from several males in her internal vesicles. Eventually, however, she is ready and once again she makes her way to the shore for the laborious dangerous task to which her terrestrial ancestry has committed her.

△
A pair of green turtles copulate in the shallow seas just off their breeding beaches.

3

The Ancient Hunters

Crocodiles, alligators and gharials

The biggest reptile alive today can grow to a length of over six metres (20 feet) and weigh over a tonne. Monsters very like it lived alongside the dinosaurs two hundred million years ago. No animal more deserves the title of living fossil. But if that name suggests that it is a rare survivor clinging with difficulty to its place in the more efficient and highly specialised world of today, then the label is a very misleading one. This huge animal haunts rivers and swamps but it is also capable of making long journeys overland in search of water and can swim for five hundred miles across the open ocean. It is found in India and Sri Lanka right across Asia to the northern tropical coasts of Australia and beyond into the Pacific as far as Fiji. It is feared everywhere for it is a man-eater. Australians call it the saltie. It is the saltwater crocodile, *Crocodylus porosus*.

Its favoured way of hunting is to lurk underwater in ambush. There is little to warn an animal coming down to drink of the danger. All it might see are two small bumps on the surface of the river and, a yard or so ahead of them, a third. They are the saltie's eyes and the tip of its snout – all it needs to detect the arrival of prey on the river bank. Its long broad back is entirely invisible to those on land for the saltie floats with its body suspended at a slight angle to the surface. It is able to do this because a compartment of its stomach, its gizzard, contains a collection of stones. In a bird, such gizzard stones help the animal grind up its food, but the saltie's stones are often rough and show little or no sign of having been ground together. They must have another purpose and it seems certain that they serve as the ballast that enables the crocodile to hold its position in mid-water in this way.

An animal cautiously makes its way down a well-worn trail through the riverside vegetation. A kangaroo, perhaps. The saltie's sense of smell is very acute. Its twin nostrils lead to nasal passages that run the length of its snout between the top of its skull and the roof of its mouth, and they are lined with sensitive nerve endings. Its eyes, just above the surface of the river, are sharp and optically suited for vision in air. They are protected from damage underwater by an eyelid that closes upwards and are kept clean by a transparent membrane that moves transversely across the eye and helps to protect it from damage underwater. Just behind each eye there is a diagonal slit – the ears. They too are acute. And the saltie has yet another sense. In the scales along the outside of its lower jaw there are sensory pores which enable it to detect the slightest movement in the water.

▷
By adjusting its buoyancy, crocodiles, like this saltie, are able to hang in mid-water.

A Nile crocodile, entirely below water except for its ears, eyes and nostrils, keeps a close watch on what is happening on shore.
▽

The saltie has been holding its four webbed feet splayed out to give it stability in the water. Now having seen its prey, it moves them slightly upwards and its body, in response, sinks slowly downwards. Muscular flaps close its nostrils and the three bumps disappear from the surface with barely a ripple. The prey, unaware that it has been spotted, starts to drink.

Below water, the crocodile gently undulates its huge tail and moves slowly towards the bank. Suddenly the river in front of the kangaroo explodes with a huge splash. The saltie has lunged out of the water, propelling itself with its legs and a hugely powerful thrash of its tail. It grasps its prey by the muzzle and pulls it into the water. With a twist of its head, it thrashes its victim from side to side and then holds it beneath the the surface until, in spite of its struggles, it drowns.

The crocodile cannot eat yet. Its teeth are simple conical spikes. They are very effective for gripping flesh but they cannot slice into the kangaroo's body for they do not have a sharp cutting edge like those of, say, a shark.

But the crocodile can wait. Even though its mouth is half-open, clamped as it is on the kangaroo, it does not swallow any water for it has a flap at the back of its mouth that closes off its throat. So it waits until its victim shows no further sign of life. Then it changes its grip. Now it tears at its underside. Eventually it opens a gash and grips the torn edge of the hide. Then, by spinning its body, it manages to tear off a strip of skin and flesh. But still it will not open its throat to swallow for it has no lips and so cannot prevent water from entering its mouth. Gripping a lump of flesh between its teeth, it rises to the surface, lifts its head above water, and juggles the meat down between its long jaws until it arrives at the back of its mouth. Then at last, its head being above water, it can open its throat and swallow the first instalment of its meal.

A crocodile's digestive fluids are extremely powerful, the most acidic known, and capable of liquefying bones and horn as well as muscle and sinew. Its stomach is small, scarcely bigger than a football but the saltie continues to feed even after its stomach is full. It

A saltwater crocodile seizes a kangaroo that has come to the river to drink.
◁ ◁

will hold the last gobbets in its gullet until in due course, digestion makes room for them in its stomach. Then, having taken as much as it can manage, it stores the remains of the carcass underwater perhaps among the roots of a tree growing on the bank above. It will return later.

◇

Saltwater crocodiles hunt with great skill and intelligence. They manage to catch marine turtles, shore birds, lizards, even other crocodiles. Fruit bats too. Bats may seem to be unlikely and inaccessible prey for a crocodile. But fruit bats drink. They swoop down to the surface of a lake and snatch a mouthful in mid-flight. Salties are clever enough to learn where the bats do this. And there they wait, hidden below the water. As a bat swoops down to the surface for its drink, so the saltie rears up from the surface and grabs it.

Salties also have an accurate sense of time to guide their hunting. During the wet season many of the rivers on the northern coast of Australia overflow their banks and flood the surrounding plains. During the dry, however, they shrink and may be reduced to little more than chains of tenuously linked pools. A few years ago, a cattle rancher here decided to build a barrage across one of the rivers that ran through his property so that he could, except at the height of the wet, drive across it. But the river in this lower part of its course is tidal and used by freshwater mullet which swim in from the sea on their way to their spawning grounds up-river. The salties know when this will be. For most of the year they are solitary creatures but now they assemble in considerable numbers and manage to suppress their mutual intolerance to wait alongside one another for the arrival of the mullet.

As darkness falls it is possible to get an idea of how many crocodiles there are in the pool upstream of the barrage. A torch scanning the surface of the water illuminates pairs of glowing lights. Crocodiles, like nocturnal mammals, have a reflective layer, a tapetum, at the back of their eyes. There are forty or fifty salties waiting in this one small pool.

Slowly the tide comes in and the water rises. Eventually it spills across the barrage and cascades down the up-river face. And with it come the mullet, flashing silver in the moonlight as they leap down to the pool in their eagerness to get to their spawning grounds. And as they do, the salties with perfect timing, leap up and catch them neatly in their jaws.

◇

Although the saltie is so well adapted to life in water, it also spends

A Nile crocodile basks in the sunshine. It is able to guard against over-heating by gaping and allowing moisture to evaporate from its mouth.
▽

some of its time on land. In the dry season it is quite capable of walking considerable distances in search of lagoons and ponds that have not yet dried out. For much of the day, it basks on mud banks warming its great body in the sunshine. This risks over-heating. A reptile cannot cool itself with sweat for no reptile has sweat glands. Crocodiles deal with the problem in a different way – by opening the mouth and holding the jaws wide apart. This gaping posture has led some to believe that there is a joint between the base of the upper jaw and the skull. That is not, of

course, the case. The snout and the skull are one. The lower jaw does certainly rest on the ground but that is because the crocodile has tilted its head and snout upwards.

The teeth, so formidably exposed when the crocodile gapes, vary somewhat in size. Although they only serve to grip, they nonetheless get damaged and worn. But they are continuously replaced. A new tooth forms in the pulp of the old tooth. As this grows, the old roots are resorbed and the old crown is forced upwards and finally expelled. It is a continuous process that proceeds in sequence along the length of the animal's jaw. In the course of its life a crocodile may replace each one of its teeth forty-five times.

◇

The first recognisable crocodile appears in the fossil record in the late Triassic period, some 215 million years ago alongside the tortoises and the early dinosaurs. By this time, reptiles with their watertight skins and shelled eggs had been occupying the dry lands of the earth for some hundred million years. These first crocodiles were, like their reptilian ancestors, air-breathing egg-laying land-dwellers. They were about a metre (3 feet) in length with long slender legs and walked with their bodies lifted well clear of the ground. A line of paired bony plates ran along their backs. These are unlikely to have served as armour, for they left the animals' flanks and bellies totally unprotected. They were an adaptation for living on land. Without the support of water, a long backbone of a large animal has to carry a very substantial load. The plates stiffened the crocodile's spine and prevented it from sagging.

Their heads were broad and their snouts narrow but short. Their nostrils opened internally on the roof of their mouth as they do in most land-living reptiles today. Palaeontologists, when inventing names for the crocodile species they discover, often incorporate into them the word 'suchus' which is Greek for crocodile (and in turn derived from the name the Egyptians gave to the crocodile god whom they worshipped). These very first crocodiles are accordingly known as protosuchians.

Some time in the Jurassic period, between 200 and 150 million years ago, some of these protosuchians took to the water. That can be deduced from the nature of rocks in which their remains are found and the other organisms – ammonites, shrimps and star-fish – that are found with them. Their legs became shorter and their feet broadened into paddles. Their snouts lengthened and narrowed. A secondary bony palate developed in the roof of the mouth forming a passage from the nostril to a position immedi-ately in front of the wind pipe so that air could flow directly down to the lungs. This bony palate also gave great structural strength to a snout that was now so elongated that it might otherwise have been at risk of breaking when its owner tried to grapple with big prey.

These new style crocodilians were sufficiently different from their predecessors for them to be given a new name, the mesosuchians. Why they moved back to water we cannot tell. The land was certainly becoming densely populated for the dino-saurs were now increasing in number and variety. But the seas too were full of big animals. Other reptiles, the ichthyosaurs and mosasaurs, both of which are now extinct, were flourishing there, feeding on the abundant fish. Even so the mesosuchians found a place for themselves in the waters of the world, both fresh and salt. This was the hey-day of the crocodilians. Their fossils are abun-dant in the marine deposits of Europe. One species became enormous with a skull two metres (6 feet) long and a total length of around 11 metres (36 feet).

The eusuchians – that is to say modern or 'proper' crocodiles – finally appear in the Upper Cretaceous some 80 million years ago. Some, judging from the length and shape of their limbs, were ter-restrial. Others spent their time both in and out of water as today's crocodiles do. There were giants among these too. *Deinosuchus* is thought to have been about 12 metres (40 feet) long or even more.

Sixty-five million years ago some catastrophic event brought the dynasty of the dinosaurs to an end. Currently, the most widely accepted view is that this was caused by a huge asteroid that

slammed into the earth creating a major disruption of the atmosphere and devastating much of the plant and animal life. Whether
this was the true reason or not is still being debated. Any explanation, however, has to account for the fact that although dinosaurs
disappeared from the land and ammonites from the sea, many
other creatures survived. The tortoises and the turtles did. So did
the small furry warm-blooded land-living descendants of the
therapsids that were the first mammals. And so did the eusuchian
crocodiles.

◇

Today there are two main groups of them, the crocodiles and the
alligators. It is easy to tell the difference between them. Look at
the animal's head when it has its mouth shut. If all the teeth in its
lower jaw are concealed then you are looking at an alligator or its
close relative, a caiman. If a particularly large lower jaw tooth – it
will be the fourth from the front – is wholly exposed and fits into a
notch on the side of the upper jaw, then the animal is a crocodile.

Alligators and caimans are almost entirely American. Crocodiles on the other hand are primarily Old World species and
inhabit Africa, Asia and Australia. The difference in their distribution lies in their evolutionary history. Their common distant
ancestors, the protosuchians, appeared at a time when the continents of the world were still united in one great supercontinent.
By the time the mesosuchians appeared, that supercontinent was
beginning to fragment. A rift appeared between what is now
Africa and South America and the eusuchian ancestors of today's
crocodilians became separated. Each group continued to evolve in
its own way and minor differences appeared between them. One
was that slight change in dentition which now enables us to distinguish an alligator from a crocodile.

The North American alligator *(Alligator mississippiensis)* once
grew to huge lengths. Monsters approaching 6 metres (20 feet)
long were triumphantly bagged by hunters in the last century.
Today, a four metre (13 foot) specimen would be reckoned
exceptional. In South America, the black caiman *(Melanosuchus*

*The dental difference
between crocodilian
families.*

*Above: the concealed
lower teeth identifies
this animal as an
alligator.*

*Below: the exposed
fourth tooth in the
lower jaw shows this
one to be a crocodile.*

niger) has similar dimensions. Hunting is not as intensive in the jungles of the Amazon as it is in the heavily populated valley of the Mississippi and there it is still possible to encounter a caiman approaching six metres (20 feet). It is the largest of all South American carnivores, far heavier and longer than the biggest of the mammalian carnivores, the jaguar.

There are also dwarfs – two species, *Palaeosuchus palebrosus* and *Paleosuchus trigonatus*. Neither of them grows longer than 1.7 metres (5½ feet). They are perhaps the least aquatic and most terrestrial of all crocodilians, living not in the open rivers and streams but the flooded forests, walking across the land with their bellies lifted well clear of the ground and their heads held high.

African crocodiles also include giants and dwarfs. The largest and the commonest is the Nile crocodile *(Crocodylus niloticus)* which is found all over Africa below the Sahara and rivals the black caiman in size, though the recorded champions are a few inches shorter. The African dwarf *(Osteolaemus tetraspis)*, like the South American one, is primarily a forest-living animal and is restricted to the western part of equatorial Africa. It grows no longer than two metres (6½ feet).

Since these two great groups evolved in their separate continents, the crocodiles in Africa and the alligators and caimans in the Americas, the picture has become a little more complicated. The saltie is not the only crocodilian that can move between fresh and salt water. Another species that is almost as big, *Crocodylus acutus* does so with almost equal ease. At some time its African ancestors must have managed to cross the Atlantic Ocean from the Old World to the New and so reached the Caribbean. Today it is found in several West Indian islands including Jamaica and Trinidad. It has even continued farther west and reached continental shores in Florida and Mexico and is consequently known as the American crocodile. There are also three other closely related crocodiles that must have made the same journey. All are rare and very restricted in their range. One lives in two swamps in Cuba, another in Mexico and Guatemala, and a third in the lower Orinoco River which empties into the Caribbean.

▷
Cuvier's dwarf caiman has a very short snout and a very high forehead. It is much more terrestrial in its habits than other crocodilians.

Just one species has travelled in the opposite direction, from the New World to the Old. This is a small and rare species of alligator *(Alligator sinensis)* that somehow or other has managed to cross the Pacific from the Americas to the coast of Asia. It now lives in the Lower Yangtze River in China. Perhaps it made the journey at a time when there was a land bridge between Asia and North America across the Bering Strait.

There is a third kind of crocodilian so different from the others that it is given a group all to itself. It is the gharial *(Gavialis gangeticus)*. Once again it is the head that identifies it. But it is very different indeed from both alligators and crocodiles. Its jaws are

The Indian gharial has long thin jaws that can be quickly snapped shut underwater to catch fish.
▽

extremely long and slender. They are so narrow that they seem hardly strong enough to withstand the great stresses involved in catching the large prey that other crocodilians regularly tackle. And indeed the gharial does not use its jaws in that way. It is primarily a fish eater and its long thin jaws are well-suited to making the swipes and snaps necessary to catch such prey underwater. Gharials are found only in the northern part of the Indian sub-continent. They grow almost as big as a saltie. The record length is 6.5 metres (21 feet). They are the most aquatic of all crocodilians and seldom leave their rivers, except when they are compelled to do so in order to lay their eggs.

Crocodiles, alligators and caimans, so similar in appearance, live broadly similar social lives. The males all establish breeding territories and mate with several females each of whom builds and guards her own nest.

Disputes are waged largely with sound. Alligators are particularly noisy. Both male and female will lift their head above the surface of the water and roar. It is a loud throaty bellow that lasts for a couple of seconds. Those who keep captive alligators say that they can recognise individual voices and doubtless the animals themselves are able to do the same.

A male establishing or maintaining a territory will bellow repeatedly half a dozen times at intervals of ten seconds or so. He also makes deep noises of a frequency so low that they lie largely

△
A male alligator produces such a deep call that his body shakes with its vibrations, causing the water to dance in droplets on his back

△
Rival male crocodiles, though capable of delivering powerful bites, fight one another by violently striking their heads together.

below the sensitivity of our ears. But you can see when he does so. He lies close to the surface of the water and suddenly the droplets on his back begin to dance and bounce, shooting several inches into the air. His whole body is vibrating with a humanly-inaudible rumble. He will also signal by lifting his head above the water and then, with a simultaneous snap of his jaws, strike the surface, making a noise like the backfire of a car. Indeed captive alligators sometimes respond with a defiant roar to such a sound coming from nearby streets.

These sounds are challenges, issued by a male seeking to establish or maintain a territory. Other males, contesting such claims, answer in similar ways. The arguments proceed by sparring with open jaws above the surface of the water. The rivals, with their mouths wide open displaying their teeth, lunge at one another. They thrash their tails from side to side making a great splash. The saltie has a particularly formidable way of arguing. The contestants lie alongside one another with their heads exposed. Then one swings his head and clouts the other with such force that the thud can be heard from many yards away.

Once arguments have been settled in such a fashion, the victor displays his dominance by swimming in a lordly, super-confident way with his head and back clear of the surface. The vanquished, on the other hand, admits his rank by keeping low in the water. He also has a special submissive gesture. If the dominant male approaches him he lifts his head clear of the water, exposing his pale neck and keeping his jaws shut. He remains motionless in this position for several seconds. If the dominant male comes even closer, then the submissive one will do his best to angle his head even higher. Such interactions do a great deal to reduce physical violence between rivals but even so there may occasionally be savage fights in which males inflict serious injuries on one another.

The male gharial develops a large growth on the tip of his snout with which during courtship he creates a buzzing noise.
▽

Unusually, this pair of Nile crocodiles have come to the surface during their long mating process.

Old warriors are sometimes seen with badly scarred legs or without an end to their tails.

Females use the submissive snout-lift to signal the beginning of courtship. The pair then spar with their snouts, swim on parallel courses, rub against one another and sometimes blow bubbles. Male caimans display to their females by lifting their heads clear of the surface and simultaneously raising their tails almost vertically out of the water. Gharials have their own unique way of courting. The adult males develop a large box-like lump surrounding their nostrils on the tip of their snouts. This has a flap inside it so that when the gharial blows through it, it makes a buzzing noise. It is this strange structure that gives the animal its name. *Ghara* means 'pot' in Hindi.

Crocodile copulation takes place in the water and mostly under the surface. Males and female can both initiate proceedings. The male is usually very much bigger than the female – often at least

133

twice her weight. If she is in the mood to accept him, she adopts a submissive posture, tipping her head upwards. The pair nudge each other with their snouts and he strokes her back with his fore-legs. They arch their backs, tip their heads up and blow bubbles at one another Then, moving with great gentleness, he uses his legs to manoeuvre her into position and mounts her. Once they have achieved union they may stay conjoined for fifteen minutes.

◇

Alligators and caimans lay their eggs in nests. The female heaps together a pile of vegetation, usually quite close to open water. She compacts it by dragging her body across the pile until she has created a large mound a couple of metres across and a metre or so high. Lying on top of this, she digs a hole, using her hind legs and into it she deposits thirty or forty white, hard-shelled eggs. Having done so, she then sits nearby, ready to defend the nest against raid-ers. She usually chooses a place where there is some shade to shield her from the heat of the sun. It is a great mistake, on finding an alligator's nest, to think just because its owner is not sitting on top of it that it is deserted.

A female Nile crocodile starts to excavate a pit in which to lay her eggs.
▽

She has to keep a sharp look out. Lizards, monkeys, foxes, coatis will all steal and eat her eggs given the chance. But she is a conscientious and powerful defender, charging intruders with open jaws and aggressive hissing if they approach too closely. One visitor she tolerates or perhaps doesn't even notice. In North America, terrapins and in particular the Florida red-belly *(Pseudemys nelsoni)* regularly dig their own small holes in her nest mound, thus benefiting from the protection that she gives to her own eggs.

Most crocodiles, however, nest in a different way. They dig holes about 60 cm (2 feet) deep in the soft earth of a river bank or in sand, in much the same way that turtles do. Gharials also nest in similar places. Clutches are large. Fifty or so eggs to a nest is common. These eggs also have hard shells. Dropping such things into a hole might seem to risk cracking them and it is said by those lucky and brave enough to watch the whole process at close quarters that the female delicately splays the toes of one of her hind legs and uses it as a kind of funnel to gently steer each egg to the bottom of the hole without damage. The Nile crocodile and several other species certainly lay their eggs in tiers and shovel in soil between each layer. They then carefully cover the topmost layer with about 30 centimetres (1 foot) of soil.

The eggs depend on the sun for the heat necessary for their development and, in the case of alligators, on that generated by the decay of the vegetation with which the nest has been made. It seems unlikely that the female in either case can do much to influence that. But the precise temperature at which the eggs develop is nonetheless of crucial importance.

The sex of a crocodilian is not determined in the same way as it is in birds and mammals. The males in those groups produce two kinds of sperm. One contains a chromosome that causes the egg it fertilises to develop into a male. The other kind produces a female. So the sex of the young becomes fixed at the moment of fertilisation. But among crocodilians and many species of tortoises and turtles, that moment occurs very much later. The determining factor is not the male's sperm but the temperature.

The eggs of all crocodilians so far investigated, if kept relatively

Stimulated by the underground calls of her hatching young, a Nile crocodile mother exposes her hatching clutch.
▷▷

warm in laboratory incubators at temperatures between 32° and 34° C, will produce males. Kept cooler, between 28° and 31° C, the same eggs will develop into females. Between the two - at 31° or 32° C – hatchlings of both sexes will emerge, though the precise ratio between male and female will vary according to the species. A fraction of a degree can make a crucial difference.

In the wild, of course, the temperature varies considerably and seldom remains uniform for long. So whether a female makes her nest in the shade or out in the open, and whether she does so early or late in the season will affect the sex of the young that eventually hatch. Even the precise position of an egg within the nest – whether it is near the sun-warmed top or deeper down in a lower cooler part of the nest – may be critical. And an exceptionally hot season, or an unusually cold one, may result in the great majority of a generation of crocodilians being of the same sex. So a rise in global temperatures of two degrees or more, that many predict will occur within the next few decades, would seriously endanger crocodilian populations worldwide.

A crocodile mother transports many of her hatchlings in a pouch that develop. in the floor of her mouth, but occasionally she even carries them between her teeth. ▽

The eggs take between 65 and 95 days to hatch. As they approach their full development, they call to one another. Shrill piping noises come from them. It is important that all should hatch together. They are going to need their mother's help to emerge from the nest and then reach the water. Stragglers would risk being left unprotected and it seems likely that these noises serve to hasten the development of those that may be lagging behind, as has been shown to be the case among some ground-nesting birds. The mother crocodile hears these noises too. She starts to excavate the nest, flinging aside the sand or vegetation with her fore-legs. Some of the young by now may have liberated themselves from their shells. Others are still imprisoned. These the mother gently takes between her huge lethal jaws and delicately presses them until the hard shell cracks and the youngster is freed. Others will already be struggling to make their way up through the sand. She begins to collect them, using her teeth like forceps. One by one she picks them up until she has as many as twenty, nestling in a special depression that has developed in

The young crocodiles in the nursery pool need to bask and will even do so on their mother's head. There can be few safer places.

7

the floor of her mouth. Then she lumbers down to the water and releases them in a shallow well-vegetated pool. She may need to make several journeys before her entire brood has been taken to their nursery.

Young caiman sit among floating plants catching insects.

Caimans sometimes adopt a crèche system. Several females will use the same nursery pool. As the young grow, mothers begin to leave until a single female is left guarding as many as a hundred youngsters in a single pool. The hatchlings have a lump of yolk about the size of a hen's egg in their infant stomachs. That is enough to sustain them for several weeks, but they are, in fact, able to feed immediately, snapping at anything that catches their eye, above or below water. Soon they are taking dragonflies, beetles and frogs. Their mother stays alongside them in the nursery pool on guard and tolerantly allows them to sit on her head and back to bask in the sunshine. The young are still very vocal. An alarm call from one of them will bring her charging formidably to their defence.

And here she may remain for many weeks until the young are able to look after themselves. Without her to defend them, they live very unobtrusively in the thick vegetation beside the water. Birds such as herons and ibis, fish eagles and ground hornbills will prey upon them. In the pools, freshwater turtles will take them.

When they are about a year old, they are usually big enough and strong enough to be able to return to open water and start catching fish. But as they grow, it becomes more and more difficult for young crocodiles and alligators to snap their jaws underwater with the speed necessary to catch fish. Some solve the problem by lying on the bottom with their jaws open waiting for unwary fish to swim close enough for them to be able to dart forward and grab them. But from now on they become more reliant on the land to provide them with food.

◇

The crocodilians evolved their basic body plan very early in reptile history. It enabled them to become successful hunters. At first, on land, they ran down their prey. Then they took to lurking in rivers and catching dinosaurs which came down to the rivers to drink. Somehow, they survived the catastrophe that eliminated the dinosaurs from the earth and when mammals began their reign, they hunted them too, doubtless using much the same techniques. They are among the most ancient of living reptiles. But none are more intelligent or have more complex social lives, and none, within their own realm, are more successful.

4

Dragons of the Dry

The lizards

◁

The green iguana, a species that has given its name to a whole group of New World lizards.

Skulls provide some of the best evidence of the ancestries of backboned animals. Body-shape is so similar in many groups that it can be of little guidance. Salamanders, newts, crocodiles, and lizards, all have similarly shaped bodies – long and sinuous, with four legs and a tail. Nor are limbs much help for they adapt readily to new functions, whether to swim or to dig, so that animals from ancestral groups often develop similar ones.

But skulls are less malleable in evolutionary terms. The shape of the constituent bones and the junctions between them, the nature of the teeth and the way that they are attached to the jaw bones, and – in particular – the spaces on the outer sides of the skulls that develop to accommodate the muscles powering the lower jaw, all these often change remarkably little over many generations and millions of years. Skulls, therefore, provide the most revealing and reliable evidence for those who work out the relationships between animal groups.

Although there are many fossil reptiles in the early part of their history that have lizard-like body shapes, there are none whose skulls allow us to regard them as direct ancestors of modern lizards until the late Permian period some 250 million years ago. However, there is one group of living lizards that closely resemble those early forms. These are the iguanians. They occur today on every habitable continent – Europe and Asia, Africa and America, and Australia. That in itself is evidence that the group

The basilisk is so swift it can run across water scarcely breaking the surface.
▷▷

143

must have become established before the great one-time supercontinent of Pangaea began to break into its constituent parts, some 200 million years ago.

The group is named after the well-known American lizard, the green iguana *(Iguana iguana)*, which is typical of them. 'Iguana' is a Carib word and was adopted by Europeans as a name for these lizards soon after the discovery of the New World back in the early sixteenth century. The animals in question are handsome creatures, growing to two metres (6 feet) in length, splendidly ornamented in most species with a fringe of flat spines along their backs. The most spectacular member of the family, a wonderfully baroque creature known as the basilisk *(Basiliscus plumifrons)* has a splendid crest on its head, but another along its spine and half its tail. These ornaments are useful as well as decorative for they help the basilisk when it runs on water. If pursued it will sprint over a lake or a river, moving its legs so fast that its toes, which have flaps, barely break the surface of the water. The crest along the spine and the tail may well serve to give it some stability as it runs, in much the same way as a tail-fin stabilises an aeroplane.

Iguanas are unusual among lizards in that they are primarily leaf-eaters. You can often see them, as you travel up a South American river, sitting in the branches of the trees that line the bank. Climb into a tree to try and photograph one and it will almost certainly leap from the branch into the water below and swim away with powerful beats of its long keeled tail. It may even dive and escape by travelling for long distances below the surface.

Lizards can swim to places that no amphibian can reach. Salt water would suck out body liquids through the permeable amphibian skin so there is no such thing as a sea-going newt or frog. But lizards, with their watertight skins, are immune to such a danger. If one of them, sitting in a forest tree or a clump of reeds, is carried away by a river in flood, it can survive for many days out at sea. In this way iguanas have arrived in all the islands of the Caribbean.

The same thing happened on the west coast of the Americas. One species carried out to sea landed in the Galapagos

▷
Above: the green iguana, like many of the larger members of its group, is almost entirely vegetarian.

Below: it is also a very capable swimmer.

archipelago, 960 kilometres (600 miles) from the coast of Ecuador, just as tortoises did. Some arrived in relatively well-watered islands where there was sufficient vegetation – low bushes, cactus and prickly pear – to sustain them. Today there are two species of these land iguanas (*Conolophus subcristatus* and *C. pallidus*), distributed between half a dozen islands. A third species, *Amblyrhynchus cristatus*, even managed to survive on a diet consisting of nothing else but seaweed and so became the only marine lizard in the world.

Other South American iguanians travelled even farther and eventually reached the islands of Fiji and Tonga where they still flourish and have evolved their own characteristic colorations.

◇

The iguanians that inhabit Asia and Africa and Australia have acquired their own particular variation of the name 'iguana'. They are called 'agamas'. Historically English names for animals are usually taken from Britain and applied by travellers somewhat indiscriminately to whatever New World species seem to them to be more or less similar. In this instance, very unusually, a name has travelled in the opposite direction – a word that was originally Caribbean is now the name of African and even Australian species. But the transfer is justified, for agamas do indeed look very like iguanas. 'Iguana' may even be the origin of the name 'goanna' which Australians also use for a group of their lizards, though unfortunately these particular ones are not iguanians but belong to a quite different group, the monitors.

African agamas are spiny little lizards that live in all kinds of habitats, from deserts and forests, to savannahs and rocky outcrops. Australian agamas – and there are some seventy different species of them – are very similar. They are known as 'dragons' by Australians. Some, the lash-tails, have extremely thin tails that are considerably longer than the rest of their body. They often clamber about in the branches of bushes. Others – fatter, flatter and squatter – live on rocks close to crevices into which they can scuttle and shelter when danger threatens.

◁

Lizard emigrants.

Above: the ancestors of this iguana travelled eastwards from South America, crossed the Caribbean and reached the island of Grand Cayman, where its descendants eventually evolved their own characteristic coloration.

Below: others moved westwards into the Pacific. Some eventually landed on the Galapagos and on those islands that are comparatively well-watered, managed to survive on cactus and other land plants.

All Australian agamas eat insects, but one has become an extremely specialised ant-feeder. It is, perhaps, the most bizarre-looking of all lizards. Its skin is raised into numerous pyramids, each of which is topped by a spine. They project laterally from its sides. They sprout from above its eyes. They bristle in a line along its back and down its tail. Its scientific name, *Moloch horridus,* is a reference to that most appalling of Biblical demons, Moloch, to whom the Canaanites sacrificed their children. The lizard, however, is no more than 19 centimetres (7 ½ inches) from its chin to the very tip of its tail and is as inoffensive and enchanting a reptile as you are likely to find.

It lives in the deserts of western and central Australia where it walks rather groggily across the sand with its spiked tail arched upwards. If it is not moving, however, you will be lucky to spot it, because not only is its outline broken up and disguised by the spines that sprout all over it but its colours of brown, yellow, black and grey match its usual background very effectively. Sitting beside a trail of ants, it laps them up with its tongue, taking one at a time – 45 in a minute, two thousand or so in a single session.

It has an odd little satchel attached to the back of its neck with a spine at each end. The most obvious explanation for this is that it is a food store. But it does not diminish in size if the animal starves, so this seems unlikely. An alternative explanation is that it has a defensive function, for when *Moloch* is threatened it points its nose to the ground, exposing its satchel. A predatory bird might therefore peck at the satchel rather than *Moloch's* more vulnerable head.

Its spines may also be defensive, although in fact they are quite soft. Whether or not they make *Moloch* an unattractive meal, they most certainly help to obtain water in the baking arid deserts where it lives. Overnight, dew condenses on the spikes and is then drawn by capillary action along tiny grooves which run down the spikes and converge on the angles of its mouth.

◇

Male iguanians everywhere use press-ups as a gesture with which

▷

The Australian moloch lizard is one of the most specialised of all lizards, feeding entirely on ants.

to declare their possession of a territory. It both frightens rivals and attracts females. Males with electric blue flanks performing energetic press-ups and bobbing their brilliantly coloured heads – magenta in some species, sulphur yellow in others – are a common sight on the sun-baked rocks around African game lodges. To emphasise the gesture, many species have heads that are extravagantly decorated with crests, helmets, and elongated spines. In the Galapagos, the males of the marine species, which for most of the year are a uniform dark black, become mottled with dull red, orange and green during the breeding season and both they and the land iguanas use this nodding gesture in their breeding rituals and territorial battles.

Anoles (species of *Anolis*), American members of the iguanian clan, reinforce their head-bobbing signal in a special way. Like all iguanians, they have a muscular tongue that forms a large fleshy lump in the floor of the mouth. This has an internal scaffolding, part-cartilage part-bone, that is known as the hyoid. Its main component is a substantial rod that helps to support the tongue and enables iguanians to project their tongue forwards and use it to pick up insects. The anoles, however, have a rather more elaborate hyoid. There is a second rod, hinged to the base of the main one, that extends downwards into the skin on the underside of the throat of the males. The anole can flick this down and forwards so pushing out a triangular-shaped flap of skin. In some species this is coloured a brilliant red, in others a pale yellow. It is so big that when it is extended, it projects well beyond its owner's chin. The vivid flash this creates can be seen from many yards away as a stab of light in the gloom of the forest.

Creep up towards a displaying male, holding a mirror in your hand, and as he catches sight of himself he will respond with repeated flicks of his throat flag. Persist and he may become so infuriated by this rival who does exactly what he does that he may eventually turn round and abruptly leap at the mirror in an all-out attack.

The American anole has its close equivalent among the Asian agamas. This is the little flying dragon *(Draco volans)* that lives in Malaysia and Indonesia. It is about the same size as an anole and it

too lives in trees. Its body also matches the colour of the bark it is sitting on so closely that it is not easy to see – until, that is, it signals to a rival male or a female by flicking its throat pouch, which in this case is a sulphur yellow. But *Draco* has an adaptation to the tree-living life that the anole lacks. The ribs of both male and female are extended into the skin of the flanks so that when they are brought forward they open a fan on either side. This too is often coloured so that it serves as a display. However, the main purpose of these extensions of the flanks is to enable the little lizard to visit every part of his tree territory with the minimum expenditure of energy. He doesn't have to run along a branch, down the trunk and then along another branch in order to see off a rival. He simply scuttles a little way up the trunk to get slightly above the intruder and then leaps into the air, splays the fans on his flanks and glides down to land immediately alongside him.

In Australia, another tree-living agamid uses its hyoid apparatus

△
Two male American anoles compete for dominance by displaying their throat pouches to one another.

▷
The flying dragon in the forests of south-east Asia patrols his territory by gliding through the branches.

to produce an even more dramatic display. The frilled lizard *(Chlamydosaurus kingi)* is a very much bigger animal. A full-grown male can measure a metre from his chin to the tip of his tail. He is at his most dramatic on the ground for if he is confronted there, he will spread a huge frill that swathes his neck. This, like the throat flap of the anole and the flying dragon, is supported by extensions of the hyoid in the floor of his mouth. In this case, however, the backward pointing rods are more numerous and much longer and project down the outside of his neck. As he opens his mouth, they erect the skinny frill that swathes his shoulders so that it becomes a kind of ruff. The wider he gapes, the more this frill is distended. It is brownish yellow in colour, flecked with lines and blotches of black and brilliant lemon yellow. The interior of his mouth is bright yellow, so the spectacle of a frilled lizard gaping at you, frill spread wide, while simultaneously hissing loudly, is quite alarming. If, however, you are undaunted and continue to advance, his nerve will eventually break and he will run for it. He rears up on his hind legs and sprints off – rather faster than you can. Eventually, if there is a tree anywhere near, he will run up it and take refuge in its branches.

It is there in fact that he is most at home. With his body and tail pressed against the bark and his frill now folded back and held tight around his neck, he looks exactly like the stump of a broken branch. The only thing that gives him away is his need to keep his eye on you. As you circle the tree, trying to see where he has got to, he adjusts his position, swivelling, millimetre by millimetre, around the branch, checking on your position to be sure that he has no need to retreat still higher up the tree.

◇

◁
The Australian frilled lizard's distendable ruff gives it a misleadingly ferocious appearance.

Somewhere in Africa at a time when the immense island of Madagascar was still attached to its eastern flank, that is to say before around 88 million years ago, one group of iguanians developed a range of special adaptations to fit themselves for life in the trees. In doing so they gave rise to the dynasty of chameleons.

A chameleon's toes, on each foot, are divided into two

bundles, three and two, each wrapped together by skin, with the claw and the last joint of each toe remaining free. These two bundles oppose one another and so enable a chameleon to grasp a twig with the firmness of a pair of pliers. Furthermore, uniquely among reptiles, chameleons can coil their tail downwards like a watch-spring and use it as a fifth grasping limb.

The shape of their body has also changed. Whereas most lizards walk with their feet sprawled out widely from each flank, a chameleon advancing along a single thin twig must necessarily keep all four of its feet directly beneath it. To help it maintain its balance under these circumstances, its body has become flattened from side to side, so that its centre of gravity is kept directly above the twig it is walking along. As a result of these adaptations, chameleons find it hard to walk on a flat surface and tend to totter alarmingly if they are forced to do so. Nonetheless, the females of many species are compelled to descend to the ground, for they lay their eggs – up to forty at a time – in holes they make in the earth.

A few species avoid this inconvenience. They retain their

◁
Like all chameleons, the panther chameleon from Madagascar has clasping toes and eyes that move independently and enable it to look in different directions simultaneously.

A Parson's chameleon lays her eggs in a hole she has excavated on the ground.
▽

◁
*The rotatable
chameleon eye.*

young within their body until the very last moment. The females can then give birth up in the trees. Each youngster emerges encased in a glutinous transparent membrane which, more by luck than good management it often seems, sticks to the branch on which she is standing or on a twig close below. The young quickly struggle free of their membranes and are then perfectly capable of hunting for themselves.

Chameleons are very territorial. Not only does an individual claim and defend a three-dimensional space within a bush, it also has, within that territory, special places for particular activities – one where it spends the night, another where it sunbathes to warm up in the morning and yet another where it regularly hunts.

As an individual perches, motionless, patiently waiting for its prey to come within range, it continually scans its surroundings by swivelling its eyes. These are conical and covered with skin except for a small aperture directly in front of the pupil. Each eye can move independently of the other and can scan through 180 degrees horizontally and 90 degrees vertically. So a chameleon, sitting among the twigs, can have one eye looking ahead and upwards while the other is looking behind and downwards. Its only blind spots are directly above and below it.

Once it has noticed prey, a chameleon will advance, with dreadful deliberation, moving extremely slowly, one foot at a time. It can, if need be, stand on its branch perfectly steadily, using just one hand and one foot. It leans slowly forward. Both its eyes are now trained on its target so it can assess stereoscopically the precise range of its prey. To help in the process, it may sway its head from side to side. If the surrounding foliage is dense, it may only be able to get a clear view of its target with one eye. But even then its assessment of range can be very accurate, for its eyes are like telephoto lenses and it can judge distance from their focus.

*A European
chameleon scores a
direct hit on a
grasshopper and
grasps it with the
muscular end of its
tongue, in order to
carry it back to its
mouth.*
▷▷

It is very important for it to get the range exactly right. The blow that is coming must neither fall short nor overreach. It must hit its target with the accuracy and power of a boxer landing a punch on an opponent's chin.

Now the chameleon slowly opens its jaws revealing its tongue,

161

a large glistening lump in the bottom of its mouth. The main rod–like element of a chameleon's hyoid is long and substantial. It tapers to a point at the front and is wrapped around by muscle fibres. The chameleon leans forward towards its prey, mouth agape. Taking aim, it moves its tongue-lump forward to the front of its mouth, like a cannon in an eighteenth century warship being trundled forward into its gun–port. Suddenly the chameleon contracts the muscles in the tongue which encircle the tapered spike of the hyoid. Instantaneously, the muscular tube slides off and the lump is transformed into a thin rod twice the length of the chameleon's body.

The front end of this rod is enlarged and muscular so it is heavy, and the spike of the hyoid only extends for about half of the tongue's length. So not surprisingly, when the tongue is fully extended, it may droop a little. The chameleon must therefore aim a little above its target to allow for this. If it hits its target, then the end of the tongue, which is sticky, will fasten on to it. A pair of muscular flaps above and below grasps the prey and the tongue then retracts, carrying its prize back with it. For most species, this will be a cricket, a fly or some other small insect. For the largest chameleons it could be a little rodent or a small bird. And then the chameleon, with grim, deliberate champs of its jaws, crushes its victim and laboriously swallows it, while its eyes continue to swivel to see what else is around.

◇

The chameleon's ability to conceal itself by matching the colour of its surroundings is famous and deservedly so. It has pigment cells in its skin which, by contracting and expanding, enable it to change its overall colour and even develop different patterns. But camouflage is not the only factor that causes an individual to change its colour. For some reason, which seemingly conflicts with camouflage, it becomes paler in darkness and darker in bright light. It is stimulated to react not simply by what it sees with its eyes but by the strength of light that falls on its skin. You can demonstrate this by holding a cardboard shape against the flank of a resting

The snub-nosed chameleon is one of the most colourful of a colourful family.

chameleon for a couple of minutes. When you take it away, you will see a pale print of the shape on the chameleon's skin.

As well as reacting to its surroundings, a chameleon also changes colour with its mood. An angry chameleon may go black with fury; an amorous one may acquire colourful spots; a submissive one may turn pale grey. The particular range of colours available for these responses depends upon the species. Some have a tendency to use blue and green. Others readily develop orange or reddish colours. And some seem to have a particularly wide range as well as, among the males, all kinds of crests, horns, hats, flaps, fringes and spikes that make chameleons some of the most spectacular of all reptiles.

True chameleons live only in the Old World, though in past centuries settlers in the New occasionally gave that name to whatever colourful species they encountered – particularly the anoles. There are some 150 species of chameleon of which nearly half, remarkably, are found in Madagascar. The biggest of all, a magnificent giant, *Chameleo oustaleti,* grows to some 60 centimetres (2 feet) long. Monsters like these can turn crimson, emerald green and black. They inflate their bodies and turn flank-on to appear as big as possible. They open their jaws wide and hiss loudly. Male Jackson's chameleon *(Chameleo jacksoni)* have three long horns on their noses with which they spar. Meller's chameleon *(Chameleo melleri)* has only one but in addition has two flaps at the back of its neck which the males erect when they fight, so that they look remarkably like miniature *Triceratops* dinosaurs. All in all chameleons can look very formidable indeed and move and behave in such an odd way that local people not only fear them but believe – incorrectly – that they are lethally poisonous.

But there are also dwarfs. These are so different from the rest of the family that they are grouped in a subfamily of their own. Most are about 9 centimetres (3 inches) long and have lost the ability to grasp things with their tail, which has been reduced to a mere stump. They live on the ground among the leaf-litter, where their

The smallest of all chameleons and one of the smallest of reptiles, the tiny ground-living pygmy chameleon from Madagascar.
▽

coloration and irregular outline make them very difficult indeed to spot. When you do find one, however, and pick it up, you may – simply out of surprise – drop it almost immediately for some species vibrate, like clockwork toys. These vibrations may be a by-product of creating a sound at the same time, but if that is so then the sound must have a frequency that is inaudible to the human ear. Alternatively the vibrations may be simply a very effective way of startling anything that might try to interfere with it.

The smallest of all, Madagascar's pygmy chameleon *(Brookesia minima)*, measures a mere 3 centimetres (an inch) long, about the length of a small grasshopper. Yet within this tiny body there are all the organs of a full-sized reptile – a backbone and a heart, a stomach and a brain. Its tiny tongue which it shoots out to collect near-microscopic flies, must be almost as thin as a whisker. It is a miracle of miniaturisation.

◇

All other lizards differ from the chameleons and other iguanians in that their tongue does not have the ability to grasp prey. For them, it is not an instrument for eating. It is a sensor with which to detect smells. As it flicks out, it gathers chemical particles from the air and then, as it retracts, it transfers these particles to sensory pads on the roof of the mouth. Meals – which in almost all species are largely insects – are not picked up by the tongue but with a turn of the head and a grab of the jaws which are armed with small cylindrical teeth.

The lizards that the classical naturalists called *Lacerta* – from which name our word 'lizard' is derived – are green, long-tailed, scaly, agile animals that dart across the rocks and buildings in the warmer parts of the Mediterranean lands. They are, in every sense, the classical lizards. And they have one characteristic which may disconcert you if you handle one. It may suddenly shed its tail which will fall and lie wriggling at your feet.

The self-amputation happens quickly and almost bloodlessly. There are several lines of weakness in the tail where the vertebrae

167

The European green lizard feeds mainly on insects but occasionally takes birds' eggs and fruit.

and the tendons connecting them can, at will, be severed. The muscles on either side contract and so do the blood vessels that normally run across the point of breakage. This talent has great defensive value. If a lizard is threatened by a snake, it may wave its tail at the snake, which may then strike at this rather than the lizard's body. If it does so, then the tail breaks away and the lizard runs off, leaving the tail segment writhing on the ground for as long as five minutes. The snake may well eat the tail – and a good meal it is likely to be, for many lizards use their tails as fat stores – but the lizard itself will have escaped. And it has been recorded that sometimes the lizard will return and eat its own tail and so reclaim its fat reserves.

After this performance, a lizard regrows its tail very swiftly, though the new extension will be strengthened not with bone like the original but with cartilage. Occasionally, the initial severance is not complete and the tail remains connected to the body by a little flesh and a fragment of skin. The wound may then start to heal while the replacement tail is growing. And this may even result in the extraordinary sight of a lizard with two tails.

◇

ke many lizards hen threatened, it ay divert the tention of an gressor by breaking its own tail and aving it wriggling the ground.

Some relatives of *Lacerta* have another, perhaps even more remarkable ability. Fifty years ago, to the incredulity of the scientific world, a Russian zoologist reported that he had discovered a population of *Lacerta* that was entirely female. He was unable to find a single male and all the females he caught were perfectly capable by themselves of laying clutches of fertile eggs. This phenomenon is known as parthenogenesis (from two Greek words meaning 'virgin birth') and is not uncommon among aphids and other insects and in some fish. But it was startling to discover it in such an advanced animal as a reptile. Sceptics suggested that the phenomenon happened because the female lizards were able to store sperm in their oviducts from much earlier matings. This explanation was eventually disproved by breeding parthenogenetic female lizards in the laboratory for up to seven generations. Later research revealed that parthenogenesis occurred in some thirty species of lizard belonging to half a dozen different families.

It seems to originate when two closely related species with neighbouring ranges interbreed. Interbreeding, of course, is not in itself uncommon in the animal kingdom but the offspring, hybrids, are nearly always sterile. Thus a horse and a donkey may mate, but the result, a mule, will not become sexually potent. This is not the case, however, in these lizards. Their hybrids can all lay fertile eggs, an ability which they then pass on to their own off-spring. Initially, this gives such lizards a great advantage, for it means that every member of the population can lay eggs, instead of only half. The parthenogenetic population therefore grows and spreads very swiftly. Its success, however, is not likely to last long. The entire population is genetically identical. They are all clones of the founding female hybrid. If the environment begins to change – and few environments are permanently stable – then without the shuffling of genetic material involved in sexual repro-duction the clones cannot produce the slight variations that are needed to respond to new circumstances.

There are around two hundred and fifty other species of lacertid very like the European *Lacerta* that can be found not only

One of Europe's four species of gecko, the Turkish gecko.
▽

in Europe but Asia and Africa. Some have scales on their tails that are elongated into spines. One or two are almost a metre (3 feet) long but most species are no more than a few inches long, and about half of that length is taken up by a long thin tail. Many are green or brown, with the male having rather brighter colours than the female. But none have those extravagant adornments of the iguanians – crests, dewlaps, or helmets. And none are able to change colour.

Other lizard groups are much more varied. One is spectacularly vocal. Indeed, its very name – gecko – is based on the calls of one species. Like the iguanians, geckos probably evolved early in reptilian history and therefore occur today in Africa, Asia, and Australia and America both north and south. They may, of course, have existed in Antarctica as well, but fossil evidence of their presence has not been discovered since nearly all the continent is now blanketed by ice.

The talkative gecko calls from the entrance of its burrow in the evening.
▽

Originally, it seems, geckos were nocturnal creatures. The majority of them still are. In the dark forests and among desert dunes at night they proclaim their ownership of their separate territories by loud and sometimes almost musical calls. They croak, quack, and cheep. The common Mediterranean gecko

(Hemidactylus turcicus) produces a series of clicks; a South American species from the Amazon *(Thecadactylus)* barks like a dog. One small species only 8 centimetres (3 inches) long *(Ptenopus garrulus)* lives in the sandy deserts of south-west Africa. It digs holes for itself a foot or so deep. As evening comes, the little lizards climb up from the depths of their holes, settle down close to the entrance and there start to call. The space in the hole behind them acts as a resonator so that the chorus of their cheeps is almost comparable in volume to the sound of frogs in a pool at mating time. They well deserve their specific name of *garrulus*. Then as night arrives, the chorus suddenly and abruptly comes to an end.

The most musical gecko singers are perhaps those that live in south-east Asia. Their calls are so familiar to the people who live alongside them that they are the basis of their local names. A small one *(Hemidactylus frenatus)* is known as the chi-chak. The loudest – and biggest – is the tokay *(Gekko gecko)*. Exceptionally for a gecko it can grow to 35 centimetres (14 inches) long and is a handsome creature, covered with shiny bead-like scales, spotted with white

△
The chi-chak gecko is about 12 centimetres long and the commonest of house geckos.

△

The biggest of house geckos, the tokay, though not poisonous, has a powerful bite and once it has fastened its jaws on something, it is very reluctant to release it.

and pink on a grey background.

Both chi-chaks and tokays have discovered that the lights used at night by human beings in their houses attract great numbers of flying insects, so they establish their territories nearby, quite unconcerned by the presence of people a few yards away. Often a single gecko will claim the entire area illuminated on the ceiling by a bulb and aggressively chase away any other that dares to venture on to it. The tokay repeats its two-syllable call about half a dozen times and then ends each sequence with a low gargle. The number of repetitions, however, varies and the local people, who are often dedicated gamblers, will sit late into the night placing extravagant bets on how many times a male will next repeat himself.

The geckos' ability to scuttle up vertical walls and even run around upside down on a ceiling was once the source of much controversy among naturalists. Some said that the rows of plates on the underside of the feet secreted some kind of glue – but no trace of it could be found. Others maintained that the pads created

173

The underside of a gecko's foot carries bands of adhesive pads.

a suction. That suggestion was disproved by putting the animals on a pane of well-polished glass on which suction should work particularly well. But the animals could not maintain their foot-hold at all well. Eventually, electron micrographs of the pads revealed that each carries literally millions of tiny hairs. Each of these splays out at its end into twenty or so spatulae that are so infinitesimally small that they are able to utilise the force that binds molecules together. This force only operates between bodies that can get within molecular distances of one another, but the hairs, being so extremely small, can indeed do this.

So the pads can make contact with and adhere to even the tiniest unevenness. Such extraordinarily close contact is extremely difficult to break and slow-motion film of a moving gecko reveals that it cannot detach its foot in a single vertical movement. Instead

Each, here magnified 2000 times, is seen to consist of a dense growth of microscopic hairs.

it has to lift up each edge so that the angle of the hairs to their attachment is changed. Only then is it able to peel the whole of the pad away.

Gecko eyes are almost as remarkable as gecko feet. At night, when the animals are hunting, the pupil is opened wide, but during the day, it closes into a vertical slit. Sometimes this is a straight line. Sometimes, however, the junction between the two halves is lobed so that, even when the pupil is tightly closed along most of its length, there are four separate pinholes, one above the other. Each of these, like any pinhole or any camera with its iris diaphragm shut down to its fullest extent, produces an image with a great depth of focus. Since so little light can pass through a pinhole this image is a very dim one. But the gecko is able to accurately superimpose all four pinhole images on top of one another on the same spot on the retina, so quadrupling the brightness of the image while at the same time retaining the great depth of focus.

All lizards protect their eyes with lids, which open and close in the opposite direction to ours. Our upper eyelid closes

The pupil of a tokay gecko's eye closes to form a lobed slit.

▽

downwards. The lizard's lower lid rises upwards. Many geckos have lids that are fused together. The lower one, however, has become transparent so that the gecko is, in effect, permanently wearing spectacles. Spectacles, of course, need cleaning and the geckos which wear them use their tongue in order to do so, lavishly licking each eye in turn.

Having been active all night, nocturnal geckos rest during the day. They must, however, keep out of the way of predators and most geckos, since they have no need to move about, put their trust in disguise. Some are so perfectly camouflaged that the human eye is simply incapable of detecting them, unless and until they move – which they are very reluctant to do. The frilled geckos of Madagascar are perhaps the most perfectly disguised of all. One, *Uroplatus phantasticus,* lives among the fallen leaves on the forest floor and in both colour and shape matches them perfectly. Another, *Uroplatus fimbriatus,* is not only coloured and patterned

177

in exactly the same way as the lichen-blotched bark on which it habitually sits, but also has ragged frills of skin around its flanks, its tail, its chin and its toes. As it settles down on the bark these fringes spread out laterally and so eliminate any tell-tale shadows.

A few geckos become active during the day, among them species of *Phelsuma*, that live in Madagascar and the nearby islands of the Seychelles. Instead of being drab and inconspicuous, they are among the most brilliantly coloured of all reptiles. Their bodies are a marvellous piercing green splashed on the back and the head with a few spots of scarlet, blue or yellow according to the species. While like their nocturnal relatives they eat insects, they also feast on nectar and pollen and so spend much of their time hidden away in the depths of flowers. The unexpected sight of one of these beautiful creatures nestled within the scarlet petals of a hibiscus is not to be forgotten.

One Madagascan species feeds not only on nectar but on honeydew, the sugary liquid excreted by plant hoppers. These insects feed by inserting their stylus-shaped mouthparts into the

▷
The tree-living frilled gecko is superbly camouflaged. Frills along its flanks, tail and chin eliminate all tell-tale shadows. It is sitting head-down with its head opposite the topmost leaf and one of its feet with splayed toes clamped to the middle of the trunk. Its broad tail extends almost to the top of the picture.

A Madagascan ground-living frilled gecko has a body shape closely matching the leaves around it.
▽

trunk of a tree and drinking its sap. An individual gecko, when thirsty, will approach a hopper and rapidly vibrate its head. The hopper, which is usually facing downwards, vibrates its tail in response. The gecko shakes its head again. This time the hopper answers by bending its tail downwards, vibrating it and then giving it a flick so that the honeydew droplet falls off and hits the gecko on the nose, from which it licks it off. It is not clear exactly how this benefits the hopper. Perhaps it is important that honeydew does not accumulate and dribble down the stem since that might well attract unwelcome insect predators. A male gecko, however, can get more from the arrangement than a drink. Sitting beside a group of hoppers, he is perfectly placed to copulate with the females as they arrive in search of a drink.

◇

Africa, Asia and Australia have another major group of lizards that includes some giants. These are the monitor lizards. They are elongated and sinuous reptiles with a long tail and a particularly long, slender and mobile neck. Their skins are armoured with small bead-like scales that have the texture of chain mail.

Like all lizard tongues, except those of the iguanians, monitor tongues are not feeding implements but sense organs. They are extremely long, deeply forked and particularly effective. With them the monitors savour the air, gathering molecules of scent, and carrying them back to a receptor in the roof of the mouth. Each branch of the forked tongue gathers its own scent molecules and wipes them across a separate sensor, so it may even be possible that the monitor can assess any difference in strength between them and thus gauge the direction from which the smell is coming. Some monitors are recorded as being able to detect carrion, under good conditions, from as much as 11 kilometres (7 miles) away.

Monitors first appeared on earth at least 70 million years ago. Some, living in Australia, eventually grew to a great size – around six metres (20 feet) long with a weight of around 600 kilograms (over half a ton). They survived until about 25 thousand years ago, so human beings, who are now thought to have arrived in

◁
The most colourful of the geckos, a Phelsuma, *visits flowers to gather nectar and pollen.*

Australia over forty thousand years ago, must have lived alongside them for a very long time and presumably have been terrorised by them. Today, however, these spectacular monsters are extinct.

The biggest living monitor is found, not in Australia, but in a small group of islets in the middle of the Indonesian chain of islands away to the north-west. The outside world only became aware of it in 1910. A Dutch colonial officer returned from the tiny islet of Komodo with stories of a population of huge lizards some of which were six metres (20 feet) long. In the event this proved to be a substantial exaggeration. The biggest specimens ever taken from the island were no more than three metres (10 feet). Nevertheless, they quickly acquired the name of dragons.

Encountering a Komodo dragon in the wild is not quite as alarming an experience as their name might suggest. You can attract one easily enough for they are enthusiastic carrion feeders. A long-dead, strongly-smelling goat carcass is all you need. Stake

◁
A water monitor gathers odours from the air with its long forked tongue.

182

it out in an open dry river bed and dragons will materialise in the scrubby bush all around you. They move slowly and surprisingly quietly, their bodies raised from the ground by their bowed clawed legs. Their bead-like eyes are small and relatively immobile and they can only look from side to side by swaying their heads. But their tongues are very informative and they will make straight for the bait.

They feed voraciously, ripping off great gobbets of flesh from a carcass, gripping it with their jaws that are armed with long, slightly backward-pointing teeth. With the exception of turtles, monitors are the only reptiles with a cutting bite that can sever flesh, and their gape is so wide that they can engulf objects almost as big as their own heads.

Records of them attacking human beings are few, sketchy and questionable. The body of an old man from Komodo's only settlement was once found in the bush, badly mauled by a dragon, but as one of the villagers said at the time, the man was very old indeed and who knows whether he died before or after the dragon appeared.

There are, however, wholly convincing accounts of dragons knocking over wild pigs and deer with a swing of their muscular tail. They then turn quickly to rip open the victim's belly or throat with their jaws. But neither pigs, deer nor any other mammals are native to Komodo or to any of the islands nearby where the dragons are found. All these mammals were introduced by mankind. So what constituted the dragons' original diet is something of a mystery. When they are young, they feed on smaller species of lizard, rodents, birds and even insects. But as they grow, they become cannibals. They chase and eat juveniles of their own species which have to take refuge in the branches of trees where the bigger, heavier adults cannot follow.

A Komodo dragon, which can measure over 3 metres in length, patrols a beach on its island home, looking for carrion.
▷▷

Cannibalism may well be an important element in their diet and the one that has enabled them to become so big. Size may be just as advantageous to an island-living lizard as it is to a giant tortoise, helping it to retain its heat at night and providing space for food reserves. On the mainland, a lizard may begin its life by

eating insects and then, as it grows, graduate to taking bigger prey such as small lizards and mammals. But in Komodo, where in the past there were very few medium-sized animals of any kind, the monitors could only achieve great size by preying on their own offspring.

The record-breaking Komodo dragon is a much prized exhibit in any zoo and there have been numerous attempts to breed the species in captivity. This has proved very difficult, with pairs put optimistically together fighting instead of mating and even injuring one another. Only recently, however, it has been discovered that this species too, like the parthenogenetic *Lacerta* species, is on occasion able to produce young without the help of males. Since then there have been a number of successes. The females, it seems, not only require no help from the males but actually resent it.

$\diamondsuit$

△
Komodo dragons feasting on the carcass of a water buffalo.

186

Australia, away to the south of Komodo, remains today the head-
quarters of the monitor lizards. Twenty of the world's thirty or so
species are found there. Some species remain small and live very
largely on insects. One, however, the perentie *(Varanus giganteus)*,
grows to a length of two and a half metres (8 feet). It, like other
monitors, is able to do something no other kind of lizard can do.
It can run very fast for considerable distances. So speedy is it that it
can and does catch and consume mammals such as rabbits.

Most other lizards cannot run for any length of time. If you are
persistent enough and they are not within reach of a refuge, it is
not difficult to exhaust them and catch them. The reason is connected with the musculature of their chests. A typical lizard has
legs that project sideways from its flanks. It walks with lateral
undulations of its body, swinging its shoulders and hips alternately
from side to side. To do that it uses the muscles of its flanks,
around and between its ribs. It cannot therefore use these muscles
at the same time to inflate its chest to draw air into its lungs. So
after it has run for a short distance, it has to stop and take breath
before setting off again.

Monitors, however, are different. They are able to expand and
contract the sides of their long necks so that their throats serve as
bellows, taking in air through their nostrils and pumping it down
into their lungs even while they are running. As a consequence a
monitor can run very fast indeed – about 40 kilometres (25 miles)
an hour, which is about the same speed as an Olympic sprinter.
And it can keep running if necessary for as much as a kilometre.

◇

Reptile eggs are easily damaged. The parchment in which they are
wrapped – which allows adults to breed away from open water – is
not wholly impervious. In a dry atmosphere, it would allow so
much liquid to escape that the contents of the egg would desiccate,
and the embryo die. The eggs are also killed if they overheat or are
seriously chilled. All lizards, therefore, take great care about where
they place their eggs. Many species of monitors bury them at the
end of long tunnels. Some, however, including the perentie, have

discovered a way of providing their eggs with an environment that remains at exactly the same temperature and humidity whatever the weather – and without any effort whatsoever on the part of the females. They lay their eggs inside a termite nest.

Termites spend a great deal of time and effort keeping the conditions within their huge mud nests perfectly stable. The shafts and chimneys inside the nests are so constructed that the heat generated by the termites in the basement of the termite hill where they spend most of their time, together with the wind blowing on the porous flanks of the nest, create up-draughts within and so maintain the freshness of the air. The nest's humidity is also controlled by its occupants. If the air within starts to get too dry or hot, they bring up water from shafts which run down to the water table in the ground beneath the nest. This labour occupies a considerable part of the lives of the worker termites, but it is essential for a colony's eggs and larvae to have a uniform environment if they are not to perish. And monitor eggs have exactly the same requirement.

A monitor investigates a termite hill in Kenya.
▽

Monitors often feed on termites, ripping a hole in the side with their powerful claws. But a female monitor ready to lay will excavate a chamber in the very heart of a nest and then deposit a clutch of a dozen or so eggs there. Having done so, she abandons them. The termites immediately set about repairing this damage to their home. They work urgently, for their young are threatened by this climatic catastrophe. Within hours, soft mud pellets have been brought up from the moist basement and used to rebuild the broken walls so that darkness, coolness and humidity at the heart of the nest is restored. The termites – surprisingly perhaps – now take no notice of these new smooth-shelled objects that have appeared in their midst.

Months pass. Eventually, the soft, leathery shells of the eggs split and the young monitors wriggle free. But they are too large to be able to make their way through the narrow tunnels along which the termites regularly scurry to reach the outside world. So they have to dig their way out of the termites' fortress.

The young of one species, the lace monitor *(Varanus varius)*,

Young monitors hatching after almost a year of development.
▽

however, do not have the strength to do this for themselves. They have to wait for an adult to come along and break into the termite hill. Females may do this when, a month or so before they are ready to lay, they start to look for a termite hill with an active colony which will take good care of any eggs that are laid in it. Alternatively, it has been suggested that somehow or other, a mother lace monitor remembers exactly where she laid her eggs and knows when they will have hatched with such accuracy that it is she herself who reappears at precisely the time her young need her help to make their way out of the nest.

▷
The biggest of all skinks, the tree-living Solomon Islands giant skink.

◇

The skinks are probably the largest of all lizard families. There are over 1,400 species of them. In some parts of the world, and most particularly in Australia, they are the most abundant of all lizards. Nearly all have roughly cylindrical bodies tapering towards a short, often even stumpy tail and are covered in scales that fit perfectly together yet allow for sinuous movement. Their bodies are thus so highly polished that handling a skink – and few are likely to bite you even though some will threaten to do so – is a physical delight. And some have legs that are so disproportionately small that they verge on the ridiculous.

One of the largest of them, the Solomon Islands giant skink *(Corucia zebrata)*, grows to over 60 centimetres (2 feet) long – twice the length of most other skinks. It has become a vegetarian and has taken to climbing trees. It has even developed a grasping prehensile tail. Alas! it seems that this evolutionary enterprise has not served it well, for now it is almost extinct.

The skinks most familiar to those who keep reptiles as pets, are perhaps the blue-tongued skink *(Tiliqua scincoides)* and its close relative the shingleback or sleepy lizard *(Tiliqua rugosa)*. Both are about a 30 centimetres (1 foot) long, with short fat tails that are similar to their heads in both size and shape. And both species have spectacular triangular-shaped cobalt-blue tongues. The blue-tongue has the well-polished scales typical of skinks; the shingleback, much rougher more heavily ossified ones. These two

▷
The Australian blue-tongued skink.

species are slow-moving creatures and shinglebacks in particular are often seen promenading beside the roads of the Australian outback.

Of all lizards, the shinglebacks seem the most sluggish, stolid and unresponsive. They sit in the shade of a saltbush, seemingly taking little notice of you, until you reach down to touch them when they will suddenly gape to frighten you off with a display of their spectacular blue tongues. Yet it has recently been discovered that these apparently lethargic stolid creatures have remarkably complex private lives.

A young male shingleback, in spring, travels quite widely through the semi-desert, seeking a partner. He identifies a female by her chemical scent, her pheromones. He may then start to follow her, trailing behind her with his head close to her tail. The pair may stay together for six to eight weeks. If she is not physiologically ready to receive him, she will keep her body close to the ground. But eventually her mood may change and she will straighten her hind legs so that the rear of her body is lifted above

△
Male and female shingleback skinks, also known as sleepy lizards, establish partnerships that are renewed annually for decades.

the ground. He then crawls beneath her and twists his body so that their cloacas meet and he is able to insert his sperm. The two then separate and go their own ways.

Unlike many lizards, the female retains her fertilised eggs within her until the young are so well developed that they are capable of independent life. This takes a long time. They grow so large that there is only room within her body for a very small number of them – usually no more than three. Then at last, after five months, she gives birth.

The young waddle off into the desert and the female resumes her lonely life. But when spring returns, an adult will once again seek out the partner it had during the previous season. Such partnerships may last for as long as two decades. If one individual is killed, perhaps, as happens only too often, crushed beneath the wheels of a car, the survivor may stay beside the body gently licking it. A coldly dispassionate explanation of this is, of course, that the bereaved has formed a liking for its partner's pheromone and is reluctant to leave its source. Other interpretations, more sentimental and anthropomorphic, might suggest that the survivor is disconsolate – if not grieving.

What can be the function of this monogamous behaviour? What advantage can it bring? Monogamy in birds or mammals is usually interpreted as being an arrangement by which a male assists the female in either preparing for the arrival of young or caring for them until they can look after themselves. But this clearly does not apply here, for the male shingleback does neither. An alternative explanation has been proposed – that it is a way by which partners minimise the risk of infection from socially transmitted disease, for shinglebacks do often carry ticks, lodged between their scales, which are vectors of various diseases. By mating only with an established partner, each may reduce the number of infections to which it is exposed.

The scientists who discovered these things made a further thought-provoking observation. They noticed that the shinglebacks they saw lying apparently comatose in the desert were in fact very well aware of the presence of human observers, no matter how still or distant those observers were. If, however, observations were maintained, not by human beings but by inanimate electronic surveillance equipment, then the shinglebacks were altogether more animated and energetic. Instead of remaining motionless for up to twenty minutes at a time and then moving away relatively rapidly to a new resting place, they were more continuously active. Perhaps there are still more complexities in a shingleback's private life – and indeed in that of many other lizards – than we yet know of.

The blue-tongued skink has a close relative – a pygmy version that is less than a third the blue-tongue's length. It was first collected from a small area of the grasslands of southern Australia but it was only seen very rarely. By 1932, it had disappeared altogether and was officially declared extinct. But then sixty years later, in 1992, scientists who were studying the shingleback happened to see the body of a brown snake, one of the common predators in these parts, lying dead beside the road having been run over by a car. They stopped to examine it and noticed a conspicuous bulge in its stomach. They opened the body and found inside the corpse of a little lizard they did not recognise. It proved to be that of the supposedly extinct pygmy blue-tongue *(Tiliqua adelaidensis)*.

An intensive search followed which revealed why the pygmies in the past had been so hard to find. They live in tiny burrows made by trap-door spiders. Whether the pygmy lizards take over vacant premises or whether they actively evict the spiders is not yet known. But it has been observed that a pygmy will choose as tightly fitting a burrow as possible – usually about half an inch across. The pygmy is then able to effectively block the entrance with the top of its scale-covered head. And even if its main predator, a brown snake, does manage to poke its head into the burrow, the fit is so tight that the snake is not able to open its jaws sufficiently to bite the pygmy.

◇

Most of the rest of the huge skink family are about the same size as

▷
The pygmy blue-tongued skink, until recently thought to be extinct, is a mere 15 centimetres long. It is so small that it habitually makes its home inside the burrow of a trap-door spider.

the pygmy blue-tongue – and happily very abundant. The one whose local name – skink – is not only the basis of its scientific name, *Scincus scincus,* but also provides the name for the whole immense group, is about 20 centimetres (8 inches) long. It lives in sandy deserts all along the northern coasts of Africa, across the Middle East and eastwards as far as Pakistan, scuttling about in the sand dunes chasing locusts and millipedes. Its body is covered with smooth overlapping scales. Its tail is shorter than its body. It has four legs, albeit very short, each of which has five toes. It can be taken as the basic model for small skink design, and the great number of species that are distributed world-wide differ from it only in minor details such as colour and dimension.

Skinks, however, seem to be unable to resist the temptation to take up a burrowing life. Several groups of them have started off down this evolutionary route and illustrate many of the stages of adaptation through which skinks must pass to attain an efficient underground existence.

Their sense organs had to change. The standard lizard device

The sandfish skink, a typical member of its family, with a stout cylindrical body and comparatively small legs.
▽

for cleaning and protecting the surface of the eye is a scale-covered upward-closing eyelid. If a lid is to fold when the eye opens, then the scales with which it is covered must be small and flexible. Some species of the *Mabuya* genus, which are widely distributed in Africa, and southern Asia, spend a lot of their time pushing their way around in leaf litter, and accordingly shut their eyes to protect them from damage. Their lower eyelids, however, have been modified so that even when their eyes are shut they can still see something. The lower lid has in its centre a single large circular scale that is transparent.

Species of *Ablepharus* have taken this development further still. The transparent scale in their eyelids is so large that it cannot fold. So like some geckos, they keep their eyelids permanently closed. Other groups, the dart skinks of Africa *(Acontias)* and the sand skinks of Florida *(Neoseps),* seem to be in the process of abandoning sight altogether, for their eyes are greatly reduced in size.

Skink ears too have become progressively adapted to a below-ground existence. A few, such as the keeled skink *(Tropidophorus),* like most lizards belonging to other groups, have ear-drums that are flush to the surface of the body. But those of other skinks are kept away from possible damage by being placed at the end of a short tube. The opening to this tube is somewhat constricted to prevent it filling with earth or sand, and in some, such as the South African *Typhlosaurus,* it is completely closed. Such canals can clearly transmit very little sound. But that does not mean that their owners are entirely deaf. They can probably detect the underground scrabblings of the beetles that are their prey, transmitted by the sand grains that press against the bones of the head in the same way as we would hear the sound of a vibrating tuning fork if we touched our skull with it.

The most obvious of the skinks' adaptations for a burrowing life is their tendency to reduce and finally lose their legs. The basic model, the common skink, which spends much of its time above ground has four legs each with five toes, like most other lizards. But even within a single genus of skinks, there can be some species that illustrate every stage in leg loss. The process, it seems, always starts with the front legs. Their toes become fewer. Then the back legs lose their toes. The legs themselves, never very large in any skink, become even smaller and change from being marginally useful as rods with which to push about their bodies, to twigs that are so absurdly small that they can serve no locomotory purpose whatsoever.

Animals with such useless diminutive legs must nonetheless be able to move around. So they change from being walkers and become wrigglers. They draw up their bodies into lateral curves and press the back of each curve against the sand through which they are moving. The technique becomes more successful the longer the body, so as the legs diminish, the overall length of the animal increases and the tail – that part beyond the cloaca which in most lizards is thin and bony – becomes increasingly thick and muscular. The result of all these changes is a skink, such as the South African blind skink *(Typhlosaurus)*, which is long, legless, and looks very much like a snake.

The Cape legless skink has become modified in several ways to suit a burrowing life. It has lost its legs and developed a stout shield on its nose. It still, however, retains functioning eyes.
▽

△
This South African skink has become extremely adapted to conditions below ground. It has lost its legs, its sight (although relics of its eyes remain) and its pigment.

Several other groups of lizards have taken the evolutionary road to leglessness though none can provide as many examples of the intermediate stages as the skinks. The European slow-worm (*Anguis fragilis*), for example, has no sign of any limbs on its flanks, though internally there are still vestiges of the bones of the pelvic and pectoral girdles to which the legs of its ancestors were once attached. If you look at this animal closely, you will realize quickly that it is not a snake for it has a face that is very recognisably that of a lizard. For one thing, it has eyelids, which no snake possesses. Its name, slow-worm, is a double libel. It is in no way like a slimy worm, being polished and delectably smooth to the touch. Nor is it slow, as many who have tried to catch one as it glides swiftly through the grass, will testify.

Slow-worms should be welcomed by gardeners for they feed on slugs, rearing up beside them and stabbing down with their heads to seize a slug in the middle of its body and then slowly engulfing it. They also flourish in captivity and are extraordinarily long-lived.

199

A famous captive specimen in Copenhagen lived for 45 years and was then introduced to and successfully mated with a 20 year old female. They further endear themselves to those who keep them by giving birth to live young, sometimes in spectacular numbers. A litter of a dozen is common. The record is currently 26. The tiny newborn babies are even more handsome than their parents for they have a delicate black line that runs from a spot on the head along the back of their silver bodies.

Slow-worms give their scientific name to a whole group of related lizards which are known as anguids. It has members not only in Europe but in Africa, Asia and the Americas. The biggest of them is a European species called the sheltopusik *(Ophisaurus apodus)*, which grows to a length of one and a half metres (5 feet) and is as thick as a man's wrist. It is rather more formidable than the slow-worm for it can catch mice and is fully capable of giving a powerful bite. Some American anguids are known as alligator lizards.

△
The slow-worm is in fact a harmless swift-moving legless lizard. Its eyes make it clear that it is not a snake for they have lids, which no snake possesses.

△
The most formidable of legless lizards, the 1½ metre long European sheltopusik.

Many anguids still retain all four of their limbs. Others have started on the route to leglessness and have begun the process, as skinks have done, by losing their front legs and reducing their hind legs to tiny relics.

Other American anguids are known as 'glass lizards' They still retain tiny stumps of their hind limbs, but they have also kept the lizard habit of chopping off their tails when alarmed. Indeed, they have taken the practice to such an extreme that they not only shed the end of their tail but sometimes break it into several pieces simultaneously. Since the tail in several species of glass lizard constitutes over half its length, the effect is particularly disconcerting, for the animal appears to have broken in the middle and shattered into several pieces.

Other groups of legless lizards retain none of their intermediate semi-legless forms that it is not easy to be entirely sure of their affinities. The blind lizards – the family Dibamidae – live in

southern Asia and extend as far eastwards as New Guinea. One species occurs all by itself away in eastern Mexico, a distribution which suggests that the group as a whole is a venerable one. Both their eyes and their ears are covered by scales. Their forelimbs have disappeared altogether but the males of some species do retain small paddle-shaped hind limbs.

Australia has yet another family of legless lizards, the pygopodids. They, comparative anatomists believe, are probably related to the geckos, though the only way you might detect this without dissecting the body of one, is to notice that it has that highly characteristic gecko habit of using its tongue to wipe its eyeballs.

◇

The biggest group of these legless lizards, that with the greatest number of species, are known as the amphisbaenians – meaning creatures that can 'go both ways', for they are so extremely adapted to a subterranean life that their heads, with both eyes and

◁
An Australian pygopodid, a legless lizard, that has become a tree-climber and grows to a length of 39 centimetres.

An amphisbaenian from South America.
▽

ears covered by skin, look very like their tails. The majority of the 150 or so species are equally divided between Africa and South America, but there are several in the Caribbean region, three in south-western Asia and even one in Spain. One genus, *Bipes*, that lives in Mexico, retains its forelimbs, but all the rest have no external sign whatever of any legs.

Most are about a foot long. Their bodies are encircled by rings of smooth, roughly square-shaped vestigial scales. These rings make them look a little like very large, dry-skinned earthworms. They also move in a somewhat worm-like way with concertina-like extensions and retractions of their bodies. They can do this because their skin is only very loosely attached to the trunk beneath. This enables them slightly to erect the scales on a band of rings so that they catch on the ground beneath. They then slide their bodies forward until the scales several rings ahead are able to get a grip on the ground and allow those behind to be released and

△
The Mexican legless lizard, has only lost its hind limbs. Its front legs are sufficiently large for local people to call it the 'lizard with big ears'.

hitched up. It is not surprising, therefore, that their colloquial English name is 'worm-lizard'.

They burrow not so much by excavation as by compression. Some have heads that are flattened from side to side, like an axe-blade. Others are chisel-shaped being flattened from top to bottom. Both kinds, however, use their heads for the same purpose. The animal drives its head into the ground in front of it and then, with considerable strength, forces it either from side to side or up and down, according to its shape, so creating or extending a tunnel. Many species, however, reduce the labour of burrowing by taking up residence inside the nests of termites or ants. There they can travel through their landlords' galleries with very little effort and there too they have a never-ending supply of food – the landlords themselves.

Their heads, because of their use as digging tools, have become heavily armoured and strengthened. Although their ears have no opening on the surface of their bodies, the animals are not without hearing. A substitute ear-drum has developed on the side of their lower jaw. With this they can detect the sound of prey in a tunnel ahead of them. They can also sense its presence by collecting its scent with their flickering tongue. Although their mouths close tightly, they have a large gape and a powerful crushing bite. They do not by any means restrict their diet to small insects and some even catch small burrowing mammals.

The true nature of these strange creatures is far from obvious. Local people, very understandably, give them a variety of names. In Brazil, the people who find them, and often their eggs, in termite or ant nests call them 'ant-kings' or 'termite mothers' in the belief that they are either raised by or give birth to the insects. In Mexico, *Bipes,* with its stumpy, broad-palmed forelegs sprouting so closely behind its head, is known as *lagartija con orejas,* the 'little lizard with big ears'. 'Snake with two heads' is also a widely used name.

Science too is a little unsure of its ground. The consensus is that amphisbaenians are descended from lizards. But from which group? Lizards with elongated bodies and a tendency to lose their legs such as skinks and geckos, have just a single lung – the left one. The right has been lost in the process of achieving a slim line. Amphisbaenians also have a single lung – but in all of them, it is the right lung that has been retained. Such a fundamental anatomical difference suggests that they cannot be related to skinks.

They also vary considerably among themselves. Superficially they may appear to be very similar but internally the different families of amphisbaenians differ profoundly. Those with axe-blade heads have very different musculature from those with chisel-shaped heads. *Bipes* has one ring of scales to each vertebra; all other amphisbaenians have two. So maybe the group is not descended from a single lizard ancestor but from several and should not be considered as a true group at all.

◇

There is yet another group of limbless burrowing reptiles. There is reason to believe that they, in fact, were the very first group of reptiles to become burrowers. They appeared around a hundred and thirty five million years ago. But having acquired many of the necessary adaptations for a subterranean way of life, they became such efficient creatures that they were able to return to life above ground. They became snakes.

5

Leglessness

The snakes

The advantages of a subterranean life seem to be considerable. Underground, an animal is away from the eyes of most predators and there it can find a reasonable supply of prey for itself – worms, grubs and beetles. Amphibians succumbed to the temptation and produced the burrowing caecilians. Reptiles gave rise to the mysterious amphisbaenians. Latterly many of the skinks seem to be in the process of making the transition. And long ago there were yet other reptiles that took to life below ground. They were the ancestral snakes.

One obvious reason for believing that today's snakes have a subterranean past is the fact that – like caecilians, amphisbaenians and some skinks – they have lost their legs. There is good anatomical evidence, however, that their remote ancestors once possessed them. Pythons have a pair of claw-like spurs on either side of the cloaca, each of which is connected internally to a single elongated bone. Some boas, such as the dwarf boa *(Trachyboa),* have several such internal relics, each of which can be interpreted as the remains of a particular limb bone.

Other features of the snakes' anatomy are also characteristic of burrowers. Their ears have no external opening. Their eyes lack moveable lids and instead are permanently protected by a transparent scale which comes away with other scales when a snake sheds its skin. The most convincing evidence of all, even though it can only be fully appreciated by an expert comparative anatomist, comes from the structure of the eye itself. This is so different from that of the eye of any other surface-living reptile that it can only be explained by supposing that at some time in the distant evolutionary past, the eye became very degenerate and could only be redeveloped by elaborating its few surviving relics.

What these early burrowing ancestors were like, we can only speculate, for there are virtually no fossils to guide us. The earliest we have is a skull that dates from around 95 million years ago in the early Cretaceous. This contains a mixture of lizard and snake-like characteristics but taxonomists are mostly agreed that the animal should nonetheless be classified as a snake. There are, however, some reptiles alive today that can give us a hint of what those ancient burrowers looked like.

These creatures are known as blind-snakes. The family is found throughout the tropics – South America, southern Asia, Africa and Australasia. That, in itself, is evidence of the group's antiquity. Some are brown, some black, some blotched. One is bright pink. A few are virtually colourless so that their blood, showing through

A pink blind-snake from South Africa. Although it probably took to burrowing in comparatively recent times, it can give some idea of what ancestral snakes looked like.
▽

their pallid translucent skins, gives them a slightly reddish tinge. Their heads are covered with large protective scales and their tails are equipped with a little spike.

They are classified as true snakes, but they are nonetheless extremely primitive ones. Like pythons, they still have relics of their hind legs – externally a pair of spurs on either side of the cloaca, and internally some quite well-formed limb bones.

One African species, Schlegel's blind-snake *(Rhinotyphlops schlegeli)* is the giant of the family, measuring up to around a metre (3 feet). But such a size is very exceptional. Most are quite small, around 30 centimetres (about 12 inches) long. One, the flowerpot snake *(Ramphotyphlops braminus)*, is one of the smallest of all snakes of any kind. Even when fully grown it only measures 15 centimetres (6 inches). Its body, which is perfectly cylindrical along its entire length with not even the slightest constriction at the back of its skull to mark its neck, is covered with small highly-polished scales arranged in rings around its slim body. If you pick one up it throws itself into loops and squirms so vigorously that it is very difficult to hold. It is clearly more intelligent than a worm, for which you might otherwise mistake it, for it reacts swiftly to the slightest touch and energetically investigates the junction between your fingers as you cradle it in the palm of your hand, flicking out its minuscule tongue.

The flowerpot snake is the most widespread of all species of snake for it can be found in horticultural greenhouses throughout the tropics and beyond, from Australia to Florida. Many horticulturalists in fact welcome it for it eats ants, termites, insect larvae and other pests. It owes its recent geographical success, however, to the fact that, like some lizards and very few other snakes, it is parthenogenetic. The entire population is female. Without the assistance of a male every one of them can produce fertile eggs.

Anatomists believe that blind-snakes are so specialised that they are unlikely to be the direct ancestors of more highly evolved snakes. The bones of their skulls have become fused together in a quite un-snake-like manner. Monitor lizards, by contrast, have skulls that are similar to those of living snakes in a number of very significant details. But whatever the precise identity of the snakes' remote ancestors might be, some elongated, legless, near-blind, burrowing reptiles, eventually left their tunnels and returned to life above ground.

◇

What tempted them to do so? Perhaps it is no coincidence that around this time there was a major change in the fauna of the earth. The dinosaurs had disappeared suddenly and dramatically, and the mammals, which until then had been small and relatively uncommon, were beginning to diversify and proliferate. For burrowing reptiles there was now an abundance of small catchable animals scurrying around on the surface above them. They represented a rich alternative to the small insects and worms which was all that could be found underground.

Many early snakes were constrictors, the ancestors of today's pythons and boas. An open-cast mine in central Germany, once worked for oil-bearing shales that were laid down around 48 million years ago, has revealed something of the range of small creatures that then populated the earth. There are hedgehogs, small grazing herbivores that were the ancestors of horses, bats and ground-living birds rather like rails and sun bitterns. And among them, researchers discovered a beautifully preserved skeleton very similar to a boa constrictor.

The ranges of pythons and boas, today, do not overlap. Boas live in South America, northern Africa, western Asia and the islands of the Pacific. Pythons are restricted to the southern part of Africa, south-east Asia and Australia. The most experienced of herpetologists, if asked to identify a living constrictor snake that he or she had never seen before, would have difficulty in deciding whether it was a python or a boa. Unless that is, the snake in question was a female on the verge of reproduction. If it then laid eggs, it must be a python. If it gave birth to live wriggling babies, it must be boa.

Anatomically, the two groups differ only in the presence of a small bone, the supraorbital, on either side of the skull above the

▷ *These two constricting snakes resemble one another very closely, but they are not at all closely related. Their similarity comes from leading similar lives in a similar environment – tropical rainforest – although on different sides of the earth.*

Above: a python from New Guinea.

Below: a boa from South America.

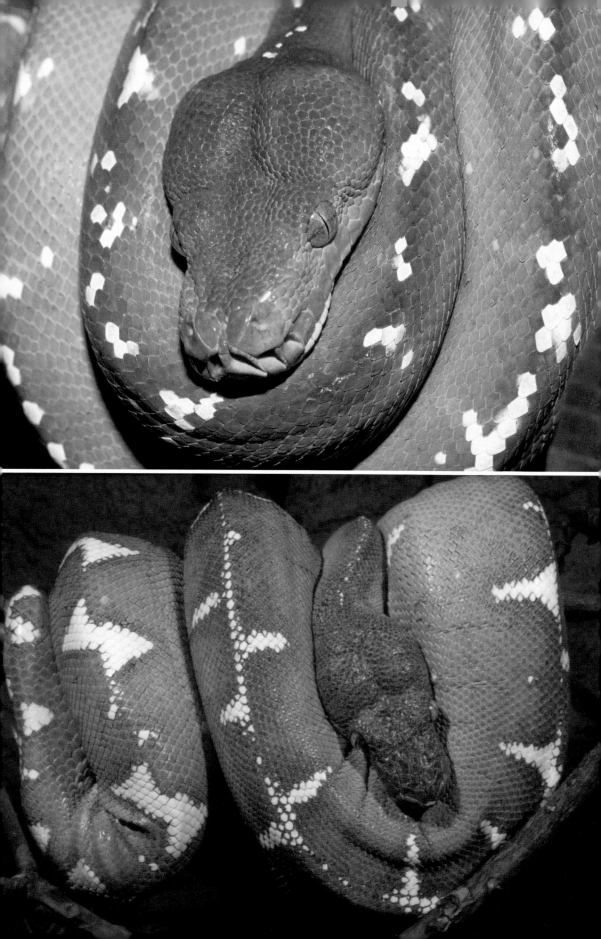

eye. Pythons have it; boas don't. But that cannot be established without dissection and to the naked eye the two families are remarkably similar. In some instances, where a species of python and a boa have the same ecological life-style, their appearance is almost identical. The emerald tree boa *(Corallus canina)* lives in the rain forests of the Amazon. It hunts mostly at night, but during the day you can find it draped in symmetrical coils over the branch of a tree. It is a beautiful green with a few transverse dotted white lines over the ridge of its spine. Travel ten thousand miles to New Guinea and you may encounter what seems to be an identical snake, with exactly the same colouring and resting in an identical posture. But it belongs to a different genus in a different group. It is a green tree python *(Chondropython viridis)*.

▷ *A serpentine wriggle, demonstrated here by an Australian carpet python, in which each lateral bend of the body can press on an irregularity on the ground, is a remarkably effective way of getting around.*

◇

Without legs, snakes have had to develop new ways of travelling across the ground. One method is to stretch the body in a straight line and then erect a band of the broad transverse scales on the underside so that they press hard on the ground. The part of the body immediately behind this band is then raised and contracted so drawing the whole body forward. The action takes place simultaneously in several such bands distributed down the length of the body and as a consequence the snake advances. It is, however, a relatively slow way of getting around.

A quicker method is to bend the body into a curved zig-zag. The snake creates each curve by tightening the muscles on one short section of its flank and relaxing them on the opposite side. These muscular contractions and expansions travel down the length of the snake producing a series of S-bends. The outer edge of each presses against any irregularities in the ground and the snake moves ahead. That irregularities are essential in order to give the snake purchase can easily be demonstrated. Put the snake on glass or some other completely smooth surface and though it wriggles as much as it likes, it cannot make any progress at all. But on normal ground, this lateral serpentine wriggling can be very effective indeed. The black mamba *(Dendraspis polylepis)* and some

A rattlesnake living in the deserts of the American south-west speeds over loose sand using a technique known as side-winding.

other snakes are said to be able to reach speeds of 11 kilometres an hour over short distances.

In tropical deserts, where the sand is both loose and very hot to the touch, some snakes and in particular a rattlesnake called *Crotalus cerastes,* have developed a method of moving at speed that must be mentioned even though it is almost impossible to describe comprehensibly in words. It is called side-winding.

It begins by the snake bending its neck into an S-bend and throwing its head to one side of the direction in which it intends to travel. The snake's body only touches the sand at the first, topmost bend of the S. But as this bend travels rapidly down the length of the snake, the snake lifts its head again and initiates another bend at the back of the neck The result is that at no time does more of the snake's body touch the sand than at the two S-bends and the snake skims across the surface of the heated ground at great speed – leaving behind a series of parallel lines on the surface of the sand at an angle to the direction in which the snake is actually travelling.

◇

Efficient movers though they can be, pythons and boas seldom pursue their prey. They prefer to wait for it to come to them. They lie motionless, camouflaged by their skin patterns to the point of invisibility.

The absence of eyelids gives all snakes a fixed stare that suggests they are examining their surroundings with great intensity. In fact, boas and pythons are very short-sighted and can only focus their eyes to a limited extent. Nor have they the muscles needed to move their eyes in their sockets. So their eyesight is poor.

Their hearing is even worse. Their ancestors lost their eardrums and the passages that led to them when they took to burrowing, so now the snakes can only detect sound by resting their lower jaw on the ground. Vibrations in the earth such as those caused by a footstep can then be picked up and transmitted along the quadrate, the bone that connects the back of the jaw to the main part of the skull, and thus reach the capsule that contains the inner ear.

But though their hearing and sight are seriously limited, many pythons and boas have additional ways of detecting what goes on around them. The scales on the upper and lower margins of the mouth carry a line of small pits. These are sensitive to heat and can detect changes of a tiny fraction of a single degree Centigrade. That sense must undoubtedly have been of great value to the early snakes in their pursuit of the recently evolved small warm-blooded mammals.

And the snakes have one further sense organ – the tongue. Snake tongues are long and forked and similar in form to the

△
The pits running in a line along the upper jaw of an emerald boa are sense organs that enable it to detect heat.

tongues of monitor lizards – another reason for supposing that ancient monitors were the group that gave rise to the ancestral burrowing snakes in the first place. Snakes, unlike lizards, do not need to open their mouths to flick the tongue out, for they have developed a small notch at the front of the upper jaw through which the tongue can slide. And as they withdraw it, so it carries back molecules of scent floating in the air which are then wiped on to twin sense organs in the roof of their mouths, one for each prong of the fork.

Thus a python, lying motionless except for the silent flick of its tongue, may not be able to see an approaching rat with any clarity, but it can sense its presence from a considerable distance by its smell and accurately track its movements from the heat of its body even in the dark – which is usually the time when such small creatures are out foraging. The rat, however, has no way of detecting the snake. There is no movement, no conspicuous silhouette to warn it. And then suddenly the snake strikes. Its head shoots forward, jaws agape. The curved backward-pointing teeth fasten on the rat. Immediately, the python throws one or more coils around the rat and begins to squeeze its victim. As the muscles of its body contract, the coils tighten. Within seconds, the rat can no longer breathe. The pressure upon it increases so greatly that the heart itself is stopped. Few if any of the rat's bones have been broken. There was no need. It died within seconds of being seized.

Now the process of feeding begins. The parts of the snake's skull that lie below the stout, rigid box containing the brain are not fused together but only loosely connected by ligaments. Thus, the lower jaw, which in mammals is a single rigid bone, in a snake consists of two linked parts that can be moved independently. As the snake gapes to engulf its prey, the connecting ligaments stretch and the two halves of the lower jaw separate. There are other flexibilities too. Half way along the lower jaw-bone, on each side, there are joints. These allow the side of the jaw to bow outwards. At the back, the quadrate bones that connect the lower jaw to the upper part of the skull also hinge outwards. As a result of all these

An African python, having killed an antelope by wrapping its coils around it and squeezing, starts on the long process of swallowing its kill.
▷▷

217

movements, the snake's gape can become considerably wider than its head.

By moving each half of its lower jaw independently and alternately the snake slowly changes its grip until its victim is held head-first in its mouth. Prey, whatever it is, is usually engulfed head-first so that it will be moved along and not against the lie of fur, scales or feathers. Having placed the rat correctly, the snake slowly works it down into its throat. Swallowing may take several minutes and with its mouth stuffed so full, the snake might have difficulty in breathing during this long time. However it is able to force the upper end of its windpipe out beside the body of its prey so that it can take air into its lungs as it feeds.

The body of its victim travels slowly down the snake's throat. The snake's lack of front limbs and pectoral girdle means that there is no bony ring encircling its shoulders through which its prey has to pass. The skin of the snake's tubular body is also elastic and stretches as the muscles of its body wall steadily force the meal down towards the stomach where the process of digestion will at last begin. If the meal has been a big one, this may take some time. If its victim had spines or even horns then sudden movement could cause a puncture of the snake's body wall. So the snake will now do its best to keep out of harm's way and avoid too much activity.

Particularly large meals stimulate changes in the snake's internal organs that are necessary to deal with the task of digestion and storage. Its heart swells by 40%. Within two days, its liver has doubled in size. Absorbing the whole meal may take a week or more. When at last the task is completed, the snake's bodily systems shut down once again, leaving only the equivalent of a pilot light activated.

◇

There are more than sixty different species of boas and pythons. Some of them are only a metre or so in length. But others are very big indeed and are the largest of all snakes. There are six species in particular that grow to gigantic proportions – the anaconda

(*Eunectes murinus*), the boa constrictor (the scientific name of which is exactly the same as its colloquial one) and four species of python: the African rock python *(Python sebae)*, the reticulated *(P. reticulatus)*, the amethystine *(P. amethystinus)*, and the Indian *(P. molurus)*.

Establishing the length of such giants is not as easy as might at first seem. It is difficult to hold a living specimen over six or seven metres stretched out straight for sufficient time to take a tape measure to it. If, alternatively, the specimen has been killed and then skinned, as has been the fate of many such potential record breakers, then the length of the skin cannot be accepted as reliable evidence of the length of the living animal, for snake-skin stretches. The very process of removing it from the flesh beneath inevitably involves a great deal of pulling and tugging and doubtless if a world record is at stake, the temptation would be not to minimise that. Some authorities estimate that a skin in the process of removal will almost inevitably become at least 20% longer than the living animal.

One of the largest of all snakes, the swamp-living anaconda.
▽

Using only measurements of living specimens, or at any rate those taken from a dead specimen before skinning, the longest snake recorded seems to have been a reticulated python that was shot on the Indonesian island of Sulawesi in 1912. It measured a formidable 10 metres (33 feet).

However, some may consider that the title of the biggest snake should go to the heaviest snake. But weight is an even more difficult dimension to establish than length. Clearly the weight of an animal that can eat a goat in a single meal will vary according to when the measurement is taken.

The anaconda is a contender for the heavyweight title as it is a very stout animal. Several records exist of living specimens that reached 7.5 metres and also had such a great girth that they must have rivalled if not exceeded the weight of the Sulawesi python. But record books also state that the heaviest living snake ever measured is an 8.2 metre (27 feet) long Indian python from Burma that lives in a North American safari park. Its weight, when last measured, was 182.5 kilos (403lbs). That was taken nearly ten years ago when the snake was 25 years old. However, snakes continue to grow throughout their lives and Indian pythons can live to be about forty years old. So presumably this one is now even heavier.

$\Diamond$

More advanced snakes, the colubrids, soon evolved to join the boas and pythons. Few of these are more than two metres long and most are somewhat smaller. The relics of the ancestral legs that the constrictors carry as cloacal spurs have now disappeared altogether. Colubrid bodies are also significantly thinner than those of constrictors. That has been achieved, in part, by the same change made by those mysterious legless lizards, the amphisbaenids, when they took to burrowing and needed a slimmer body. They modified their lungs. Instead of a pair lying side by side, one lung has been slimmed and elongated and the other reduced to a functionless relic. The amphisbaenians suppressed the right lung. The colubrids suppressed the left.

Today the colubrids are the most numerous of any group of snakes. There are over one and a half thousand species of them. They are found in every continent, except Antarctica, and in every kind of habitat, except the coldest. The American whip snakes *(Coluber* species*)* from which genus the whole family gets its name, are large creatures growing to a couple of metres or so in length, that actively chase mice, lizards and sometimes other smaller snakes. A European relative, the western whip snake *(Hierrophis viridiflavus)* can be found as far north as snorthern France. Another colubrid, the commonest of all European snakes, the grass snake *(Natrix natrix)* has a range that extends even further north into Scandinavia. It is more of a water-living creature than its name suggests, and spends much of its time swimming in ponds and rivers searching for frogs, newts, tadpoles and small fish which are its main diet.

The European grass-snake is an excellent swimmer and hunts predominantly frogs, though it also eats newts, fish and even small mammals.

But colubrids of one kind or another have made their homes in every kind of environment. The sand snake *(Psammophis leightoni)* wriggles its way across desert dunes seeking lizards. Tentacled

*The tentacled snake
hunts for fish,
hanging above the
water from the
branches of the
mangroves in the
swamps of south-east
Asia. The function
of its strange
tentacles is
uncertain.*

snakes *(Erpeton tentaculatus)* hang by their tails from trees over-hanging rivers to catch fish in the water below and bird snakes *(Pseustes species)* wind their way down branches to pluck young chicks from the nests that weaver birds hang from the very ends.

Snakes swallow their prey whole. But there is one exception. This is the crab-eating snake *(Fordonia leucobalia)* which lives in the mangrove swamps of the Malaysian peninsula. The crabs it feeds on are not only, like all crabs, armour-plated, but also covered in spines. The problem facing the snake is therefore a considerable one. Without limbs it cannot hold the crab and break it open. Nor can it chew the crab since its teeth are only able to pierce and hold prey. It is as if we tried to tackle a lobster with our hands tied behind our backs.

Fordonia starts by stalking a crab and striking not with its mouth but with its whole head, so that the crab is pinned down on the mud by the underside of the snake's lower jaw. Next the snake loops its body so that it lassoes the crab. Then, holding it tight, it bends down its head and tears the crab apart with its teeth.

Many colubrids have taken to the trees. Twig snakes *(Thelatornis species)* are thinner than pencils but have very long bodies. Entwined in the branches of a bush they are indistinguish-able from the twigs that surround them – unless you happen to spot their bright glittering eye. The boomslang *(Dispholidus typus)* whose colloquial name in Afrikaans means simply 'tree snake' is very variable in colour – black, brown, grey – but often a superb emerald green. It can move through the tangled branches of bushes at extraordinary speed and with marvellous grace. So secure is it that sometimes, having spotted prey, it will suddenly stop with a considerable length of the front part of its body unsup-ported in mid-air, while it focuses on likely prey – a lizard or a bird.

*The body of a twig
snake is often so
close in diameter to
the branches through
which it climbs that
it may be difficult to
distinguish which is
plant and which
reptile.*

The paradise flying snake *(Chrysopelea paradisi)* of the south-east Asian rainforest has become specialised in a way that parallels the gliding technique of the little flying lizard *(Draco volans)* that lives in the same trees. It is a small and particularly beautiful species with elegant golden lines across its head and yellow and scarlet

scales scattered among the black ones that cover most of its body. It can climb vertical trunks at great speed using the standard serpentine method of pressing the curves of its body against roughnesses of the bark.

But it has an even more remarkable way of travelling. Having reached the canopy it may decide that it would prefer to look for prey in another tree. It races along a branch and, on reaching the end, launches itself into the air. As it leaves the branch, it maintains its lateral coils so that its silhouette approximates more to a squarish rectangle than a straight line. At the same time it flattens its body and pulls the margin of its flanks downwards so that its underside becomes visibly concave and traps the air beneath it, so slowing its fall. It is able to do this particularly effectively because the transverse scales on its underside have hinges at each end that allow their tips to be bent downwards. In this way a flying snake can easily travel twenty or thirty yards horizontally from its take-off point.

△
The green mamba is a large snake, growing to over 2 metres long. It can travel at considerable speed through branches seeking small mammals, birds and roosting bats.

▷
The paradise tree snake is an extremely adept tree climber but has a special way of moving from one tree to another.

It can even, to some degree, steer while in the air. We once, in Borneo, started to film such a flight. Having captured a flying snake in the forest we took it to a water-tower in the forestry station where we were staying. In order to be sure of its exact take-off point and thus focus our cameras on it from the very beginning of its glide, we tied one end of a short plastic hose to the tower rail and then inserted the snake head-first into the other. *Chrysopelea* came out of the far end, executed a splendid glide and landed on the lawn of neatly clipped grass that surrounded the tower. We immediately caught it and took it back up the tower so that we might get a second rather tighter close-up shot. The same thing happened. So we took it back for a third flight. But this time – seemingly – it had assessed the situation. Somewhat to one side at the edge of the lawn there was a large and dense clump of very tall bamboo. As the little snake glided down for the third time it suddenly executed a neat left-hand turn and

△
In mid-air, a paradise tree snake draws its ribs forward to broaden its body as much as possible, and so increase its air-resistance and gliding ability.

landed deep in the bamboo clump where we could not possibly re-catch it.

◇

Some species have evolved special equipment to help them catch particular prey. Wolf snakes *(Lycodon* species*)* have enlarged front teeth which help them grip the shiny polished bodies of skinks. Shovel-nosed snakes *(Chionactis occipitalis)* have a sharp-edged scale on their noses with which they dig up lizard eggs.

Another rainforest tree dweller, an African colubrid, *Dasypeltis scabra,* has a particularly specialised way of procuring its food. It eats nothing but birds' eggs. Although it is about a metre in length, its neck is scarcely thicker than a human finger. Yet it will tackle eggs the size of a chicken's. The two halves of its lower jaw are connected by skin folded like a concertina so that the joint is extensible. The snake can therefore put its mouth around an egg that is three or four times the diameter of its own head.

Once the egg is engulfed, the snake is able to push it farther and

An egg-eating snake tackles a meal many times the size of its head.
▽

farther down its oesophagus by contracting the muscles of its body wall. The vertebrae from the twenty-first onwards have downward spines that project through the oesophagus wall. As the egg moves into this section, the snake arches its backbone upwards to accommodate the egg, but when the front of the egg reaches vertebra number 29, the snake contracts the whole of this part of its body. This crushes the shell into a multitude of pieces, though they are still connected by the membrane that lines the shell internally. The vertebral spines then slit this membrane so that the contents are expelled and pass down to the stomach. It maintains the pressure until the egg's contents have been totally emptied. Then it regurgitates the fragmented mass of shell, still mostly connected by the membrane and – often – takes a rest after its exertions, curled up in the nest of the bird it has just robbed.

△
Once an egg is well down the egg-eating snake's throat, the snake crushes it by contracting its body muscles, pressing the shell against spines that point down from this section of its backbone.

◇

230

Most colubrine snakes are non-poisonous. They rely on squeezing and mechanical chewing to kill or subdue their prey. But not all. About a third of the fifteen hundred species have venom and at least one of these, the boomslang, can give a bite that can kill a human being.

The ability to produce venom may well be something that the snakes have inherited from their remote surface-living ancestors. Skull structure and the character of the tongue suggest that those ancestors were monitors. And some monitors, the Komodo dragon among them, have glands in their mouths that produce a poisonous saliva. More impressive still, the only two contemporary lizards that have a truly lethal venom are close relations of the monitors. They are the Gila monster (*Heloderma suspectum*) and a very similar species, the Mexican beaded lizard (*Heloderma horridum*).

These two reptiles have an ancient ancestry. Fossils of creatures

that seem virtually identical have been found in mid-Cretaceous rocks that were deposited some hundred million years ago. They are big creatures. The beaded lizard can grow to a length of nearly a metre and the Gila monster is almost as large. Their bodies are covered with stud-like scales that lie edge to edge on the skin and do not overlap like tiles on a roof as they do on many other lizards. These scales also carry warnings of their owner's dangerous nature, for they are conspicuously coloured pink, black and yellow.

△
The beaded lizard, like its close relative the Gila monster, has a deeply forked tongue, which, together with its possession of venom, suggests a distant relationship with snakes.

The venom these lizards produce comes from enlarged salivary glands on either side of the lower jaw. A duct discharges it into the space between the lower lip and the jawbone and capillary action draws it up grooves on the lizard's teeth. When one seizes its victim – a small rodent or a nestling bird – it keeps its jaws clamped firmly shut for some time, allowing the venom to flow into the wounds it has inflicted. This venom is sufficiently powerful to kill a small vertebrate and to cause a human being great pain.

There are even a few records of people dying as a consequence of a bite.

Some colubrine snakes also produce their venom from modified salivary glands. These are not, like those of the Gila monster, in the lower jaw but the upper and they lie right at the back of the mouth close to the angle of the jaws. The fangs closest to them are somewhat larger than the rest of the teeth and are thus able to envenom what they can reach. These snakes are therefore called 'back-fanged'. When they strike, they hold on for some time, often working their jaws from side to side in order that their back fangs reach what they have seized and the venom has time to penetrate the wound. However, they can only kill prey that is small enough to fit deep into the mouth and to most large animals, including human beings, most back-fanged snakes are not dangerous. Their venom is comparatively feeble and their means of delivering it too limited.

◇

That, however, is not the case for another large group of more advanced snakes. These are the elapids. They include the kraits, the mambas and the cobras – and they are very dangerous indeed. Cobras deliver their venom with great efficiency. The glands that produce the venom are separated from those that secrete saliva and are greatly enlarged. One lies behind each eye and in some species stretches back along the upper jaw and down the neck. Ducts leading from each gland run forward along the jaw and empty into a pair of fangs not at the back of the mouth but at the very front. The channel running up the tooth is not a simple open groove. The sides of it have grown over and are fused together so that each fang has become a closed tube. The opening of this tube, near the tip, is oval in shape and slightly ridged so that the fang has a cutting edge. When the snake strikes, the muscle that pulls the mouth shut also simultaneously compresses the gland so that venom spurts out from the tip of the fang. Several species of cobra warn those that might interfere with them that they possess a lethal bite by inflating the skin on either side of the neck into a

hood. In the case of the Egyptian cobra *(Naja naja)* this is prominently marked with a black blotch surrounded by white.

However, a number of species of cobra – including the
Mozambique *(Naja mossambica),* the black-necked *(Naja nigricollis)*
and the rinkhals *(Hemachatus haemachatus)* – have developed
another use for their venom. They use it not only to kill their prey
but to deter attackers without even biting them. They are spitters.
The opening at the end of each of their fangs is not elongated but
somewhat more circular and placed not at the tip but a little distance from it and on the front surface.

Approach one of these snakes and it will first rear up and
slightly distend the sides of its neck into a hood. At this stage you
would be very well advised to retreat. If, however, you are wearing goggles, you can advance a little closer. By the time you are a
couple of paces away, the snake may well decide that you are
quite close enough. It lifts its head, opens its mouth and squirts
two jets of venom from the apertures in the front of its fangs. As it
does so, it turns its head slightly from side to side, so that a

◁
An Egyptian cobra gives warning of its lethal capabilities by distending its prominently marked hood.

The spitting cobra squirts venom from a small aperture at the bottom of each of its fangs and aims with considerable accuracy at the eyes of an aggressor.
▽

horizontal band of venom droplets appears on your goggles directly in front of your eyes. Its aim is remarkably accurate. Had you not been wearing protection you would immediately be blinded and experiencing the most intense pain in your eyes. In some cases, people have lost their sight permanently.

◇

Coral snakes also belong to the family, the elapids, that contains the cobras. Their venom is equally potent and they give warning that this is so in a very conspicuous, blatant way. They are among the most vividly coloured of all snakes, banded with black, yellow and pink. Indeed, they are called coral snakes not because they live among coral but because of their spectacular colour. There are some sixty different species of them. They are not large – the biggest from the Amazon can, it is true, grow to a length of 1.5 metres but most are only a foot or so long. Warning off an attacker benefits the snake as well as the intruder. Venom is precious. It takes a lot of energy from the body to manufacture it. It is not to be wasted.

But there are other snakes which in size, shape and general colouration match the appearance of coral snakes very closely but which are not in the least poisonous. They are mimics. The phenomenon of mimicry was first noticed – and explained – among butterflies. But these snakes exemplify it in an even more dramatic way. Just such a pair are Allen's coral snake *(Micrurus alleni)* and the neck-banded snake *(Scaphiodontophis annulatus)*. The first is an elapid with a particularly poisonous bite; the second a back-fanged snake that is not in the least dangerous.

There is, in fact, a difference between the two if you look carefully. The order in which the coloured rings are placed is not the same. But how do you remember the details when you encounter a brightly coloured banded snake in the wild? Perhaps the best thing to do is to react in the same way as the mimicry theory suggests that you probably will – that is to say, to leave it strictly alone, whatever it is. But if you are in Florida at the time and you feel impelled to investigate further and contemplate picking up

◁
Although the king snake (above) at first sight resembles the lethally poisonous coral snake (below), it is quite harmless.

The key to detecting the difference between the two lies in the order of the colour rings. If red is next to black the snake is harmless. If red is next to yellow, the snake is very dangerous.

A yellow-lipped sea-krait hunts fish, with a venom so powerful that it kills almost instantaneously, a valuable quality when hunting swift-swimming ocean-going fish.
▷ ▷

the snake in question, then you may get guidance from a local mnemonic rhyme. 'Red and yellow, kill a fellow. Red and black, venom lack.' Whether you have sufficient confidence in the accuracy of your memory to risk your life on it, is of course, another question. It should also be added there are about seventy five different species of small snakes with very similar brightly coloured bands and the mnemonic by no means applies to them all.

One group of elapids, closely related to the cobras, can indeed be found among coral. These are true sea-snakes. You can see them in the Western Pacific and Indian Ocean working their way along a reef, investigating every crevice and cranny, hunting for gobies and eels. They usually work in depths no greater than 30 metres (100 feet) but they have been recorded at more than 150 metres (500 feet) below the surface. Most remarkably, huge numbers of them, usually the yellow-bellied sea-snake *(Pelamis platinus)*, occasionally form great slicks floating on the surface of the sea that extend for miles and contain many thousands of individuals.

Sea-snakes have become adapted to a sea-going life in many ways. The end section of their bodies has become flattened and oar-like so that the standard serpentine wriggle enables them to swim at considerable speed. They have a valve at the front of their mouths that enables them to close the small notch through which they extend their tongue. Their nostrils too have valves and their single lung has become greatly extended. Its end section has a muscular wall so that during a long dive, they can pump the air from the back of their lung to the more absorbent front part. Their bodies inevitably absorb a certain amount of sea-water, but they have a special gland at the base of the tongue that secretes salt which they remove as they flick their tongue. Some of them are still tied to the land for they have to return to lay their eggs. Another group, however, spend their entire lives at sea for they are able to give birth to live young.

Sea-snake venom is one of the most powerful produced by any snake, yet paradoxically, they very seldom bite when handled. In this, they are not typical of their family. The elapids as a group are

240

△
The yellow-bellied sea-snake has a broad oar-like end to its body, which enables it to swim at speed.

The most formidable of all snakes, the giant king cobra, grows to a length of 6 metres and can rear up to the height of a man and confront him, eye-to-eye. It feeds on other snakes.
▷ ▷

dangerous animals. They include the most terrifying of all snakes, the king cobra *(Ophiophagus hannah)*. This species fully deserves its regal status. It is easily the biggest of all venomous snakes, reaching a length of 5.5 metres (18 feet). It is thought to be among the most intelligent of all reptiles. If threatened it rears up almost to the height of a man, spreads its neck into a hood and growls loudly. It is the only snake to make a nest of leaves for its eggs. This it will actively defend against intruders of all kinds, including elephants which it can kill with a bite on their trunk. And its main food is other snakes – pythons, rat snakes and even other lesser cobras.

◇

The most elaborate way of delivering venom has been evolved by yet another family of snakes, the vipers. These include, as well as several different species of viper, such feared creatures as the bush-master, the fer-de-lance, puff adders and rattlesnakes. The fangs of

241

A Gaboon viper exposes its huge fangs.

a king cobra are little more than a centimetre in length. The Gaboon viper *(Bitis gabonica)*, by contrast, which is less than a third of the king cobra's size, has fangs four times longer. They are so big that if they were fixed in their sockets the snake would be unable to shut its mouth. But they have hinges at their base so that they can fold back and lie, each sheathed in a scabbard of mucous membranes, along the roof of the mouth. Furthermore, a viper can control every element in the movement of its fangs. It can open its mouth until its gape is effectively 180 degrees wide and not even erect its fangs. It can also bite without discharging any venom. And it can bring each fang forwards separately or together. The fangs themselves are shed every six to ten weeks and replaced with new ones that appear alongside the old.

Allied with this great refinement in their weaponry, one sub-group of this family, the pit vipers, have an exceedingly sensitive system for prey detection – a pair of deep pits on the side of the face between the nostril and the eye. They are larger than the nostril but smaller than the eye and lie in indentations of the upper jawbone. They are equivalent to the sense organs that line the lips of some pythons but have a much more elaborate structure.

Each pit is divided into two by a membrane two-thirds of the way down its length. This is exceedingly thin – a mere 0.0025 millimetres – and carries within it a mesh of nerve cell endings. It has been known for a long time that these pits enable the snake to detect a very slight change in temperature such as might come from the body of a small mammal within half a metre of it. More recent work suggests that these sense organs can do more than that. They enable the snake to perceive the shape of the body that is emitting heat. The fact that the sensitive membrane is placed some distance down a narrow pit and that there are two such pits suggests that they give what might be described as a 'binocular' sense of heat, enabling the snake to locate quite precisely the place from which the warmth comes. This must more than compensate these night-time hunters for their inefficient eyes, for these pits will be at their most informative at night when the difference between the temperature of a mammal's blood and its

Pit vipers, like this south-east Asian white-lipped species, have a deep pit between each eye and nostril that can detect minute differences in temperature.

245

surroundings is at its greatest.

Witnessing a kill by a viper under natural conditions in the wild is a very rare experience indeed. We decided to attempt to film a timber rattlesnake *(Crotalus horridus)* hunting in the woodlands of upper New York State. This particular species during the summer tends to feed mostly at night. We found one lying curled beside a boulder in the underbrush. It was barely more than a metre (3 feet) long and lying neatly coiled with its neck drawn back into an S-curve and its head resting on its flank. Its back was patterned with large brown chevrons placed with such regularity along its length that you might think they would have made it conspicuous. But not so. It was almost invisible. Without the help of scientists who had been studying the species in this particular patch of woodland for many years we would have been lucky indeed to find it. It lay quite immobile while, a few yards from it, we set up an electronic camera specially adapted to produce pictures in minimal light. To this we attached sensors that would detect any major movement and switch on a video recorder. This would run while there was movement of some kind in the picture and for four minutes after that movement had ceased – and then switch itself off.

We did this for several nights without managing to record anything of any significance. But on the morning after the fourth we were lucky. The snake we had chosen was waiting curled up alongside a dead branch that crossed the picture diagonally. It was investigating the branch and that action had turned on the camera. With neck outstretched, it flickered its tongue along the whole length of the branch and then up a little leafy sapling that was growing alongside. No doubt it was checking whether there was any sign of prey having recently passed that way. Most rodents use the same trails as they run across the forest floor and rattlesnakes, having identified such a trail with their sensory tongues, deliberately choose to wait in ambush alongside one. The snake settled itself back with its neck in an S-bend and its head resting on its flank an inch or so from the branch's middle section. The camera switched itself off.

Once again, the recorder switched on. This time it had been

▷
A timber rattlesnak
from the woods of
North America.

activated by a mouse that was sitting at the far end of the dead branch. It looked round inquisitively, twitching its whiskers. The snake, a mere foot or so from it, remained as motionless as a stone. The mouse was not likely to have seen the snake for the night was a very dark one. To us it seemed obvious – but our night camera was giving us a very privileged view.

Having apparently reassured itself that all was well, the mouse sauntered down the branch and trotted right past the snake. To our surprise, the snake remained immobile and the mouse disappeared. Seconds passed. The snake flickered its tongue and readjusted the position of its head. It was as if it had now noted the exact route that mice followed through this patch of ground and was making the last refinements to its attacking position. Everything was still for the prescribed four minutes. Then the recorder switched itself off and the screen went blank.

But then it started once again. Another mouse was standing in exactly the same position as the first at the end of the branch. It too started to walk down the log – and in a flash the snake struck.

In the slow-motion replay we could see its mouth gaping widely, its two needle fangs projecting directly forward. They stabbed the mouse in the flank and in the same instant withdrew. The mouse leapt into the air, in a high curving somersault and landed a foot away from the snake. As it hit the ground, it convulsively jerked its legs so that once more it arced through the air. Once again it landed. But this time it fell in a patch of long withered grass and we could no longer see it. The snake had curled itself up again in its original position. Once more the camera came to the end of its predetermined run and switched itself off.

When it started again, it was the snake that was moving. With slow fluid grace, it unwound its coils. Its tongue flicked back and forth, presumably seeking the mouse's scent. It glided into the grass and disappeared. Had the mouse in its death throes moved yet further away? We could not see. The withered leaves twitched for a few seconds and then the rattlesnake reappeared, holding the mouse head-first in its jaws. It was stone dead.

Slowly and deliberately, with great gulps and yawns and facing the camera, the snake began to swallow the mouse. It took a minute and twenty seconds before the tip of the mouse's tail disappeared between the snake's jaws and it was able to shut its mouth.

◇

Just as cobras inflate their hoods and, in some species, spit to warn off those that might interfere with them, so pit-vipers vibrate their tails as a warning. This, particularly if the snakes are in contact with dried stems or leaves, creates a buzzing noise. Rattlesnakes have elaborated the technique. The tail of a newly-hatched baby rattlesnake ends in a little spherical knob. This is shed when the infant snake moults for the first time a few days after it has hatched. It is replaced by a larger button-shaped scale which hardens into a hollow sphere. When the next moult occurs, the skin elsewhere is shed but although the terminal scale loosens, it is not cast off and remains loosely linked to the old one. These hollow scales are each divided into two lobes by a slight constriction

A Gaboon viper, having killed a wood mouse, almost instantaneously with one stab of its fangs, collects the dead body and prepares to eat it.
▽

across its centre. When the rattlesnake vibrates its tail, these hollow scales rattle, making a loud characteristic sound that can be heard from 30 metres away. The vibration is so rapid – around 50 times a second – that to the human eye the tail is just a blur. The rattler itself, of course, cannot hear the sound for, like all snakes, it is deaf. The advantage of the noise is to warn off its enemies and animals of all kinds, on hearing it, retreat or at least approach it with some caution. So should human beings. No one except the deaf can say that they were not warned. So the rattlesnake avoids the unnecessary expenditure of valuable venom.

The hollow scales at the end of a rattlesnake's tail produce a warning rattle when shaken. Since a scale is added every time the snake sheds its skin, the size of the rattle gives an indication of its owner's age.

It is sometimes thought that the number of component scales at the end of an individual tail indicates the exact age of its owner in years. This is not the case, firstly because in the early part of its life a rattlesnake may shed its skin not once but three or four times a year; and secondly because when the rattle is very long, its end may break off. Even so, mature specimens with thirteen components to their rattle have been found in the wild. In captivity, where the snakes lead more protected lives and are less likely to break the end of their rattles (which are usually a source of much pride to their keepers), specimens with eighteen components are not exceptional.

Rattlesnakes, like many other vipers and colubrids, dance. Two males draw themselves alongside one another and rear up vertically so that almost half of the body is in the air. They sway close to each other until one manages to get its neck around its rival's. It then tries to bear down on its rival with such strength that eventually it slams it on the ground. There they continue to wrestle until they rear up again for another trial of strength. The performance may continue for an hour or so. The battle is not part of courtship since both participants are males. Nor is it a fight over territory for individual males may wander widely and do not hold individual home grounds. It is possible that it is a dispute over access to a female. Some observers of such conflicts have failed to find a female nearby but that could have been because she has moved away to leave the males to settle their fight and will receive the victor later elsewhere.

Courtship is conducted horizontally. The male crawls alongside the female, nudges her with his head and flicks his tongue over her. At the same time, he curls his tail underneath her. Eventually, she raises her tail and the male everts his penis.

The male snake's reproductive organ, like that of a male lizard, consists of a pair of blind tubes that develop on the wall of the cloacal passage, one on each side. As courtship proceeds, blood floods into a sinus that surrounds one of these tubes and builds to such a pressure that the tube is forced out of the cloaca like the finger of a rubber glove. For a long time it was believed by anatomists that these two organs had to be clamped together to form a tube down which the sperm could travel. Each therefore was referred to as a hemi-penis. The term is still used, rather misleadingly, even though it is now recognised that each is complete in itself and can act independently of the other. In snakes, the situation is made rather more complicated by the fact that some species

have hemi-penises, each of which is deeply forked. So an inno-
cent eye, on seeing such things exposed, might imagine that the
male snake in question had four penises. Furthermore, each is
bedecked with rows of spines, corrugations and folds of skin,
technically known as flounces. These vary in their pattern from
one species to another. Each hemi-penis, when distended, projects laterally. A male snake only everts one at a time so he is able,
without difficulty, to connect with the female, no matter on
which side of him she is lying. The spines at the base fasten to her
cloacal wall and the folds and other irregularities at the end fit
neatly around the opening of the tube within the female's cloaca
that leads to her oviduct.

Once union has been achieved, the two may lie together for
many hours, on occasion for over twenty-four. The male's sperm
is discharged and conveyed to the female along a groove in the
outside of the wall of the hemipenis. It may either fertilise her
eggs immediately or she may keep it in a separate vesicle within
her body where it can remain viable for several months.

The females of almost all species of rattlesnake retain their eggs
inside the oviduct until their development is completed. Then
one by one, and helped by muscular contractions of the female's
body, they begin to emerge from the female's cloaca. Most are still
enclosed by a membrane but they quickly break free and are ready
to grab a meal for themselves almost immediately. The female
rests for half an hour or so between each delivery until a litter of a
dozen or so has been produced. The young stay close to their
mother for the first week of their lives and she actively defends
them should danger threaten. Then, when they have completed
their first moult, they leave her to take up independent lives.

◇

The rattlesnake represents the very acme of serpentine sophistica-
tion. It has superlative sensing organs that exploit infra-red and
chemo-sensory stimuli to enable it to locate its prey. It is armed
with one of the most powerful of all venoms with which it can
inject its victims with surgical precision. It is long-lived and

produces its young fully formed and immediately capable of fending for themselves.

But it has one vulnerability, one way in which human beings who see rattlesnakes as a threat to their own dominance are able to attack it. In North America, in the northern part of the rattlesnake's range, winters can be so severe that a cold-blooded snake cannot remain active. So many species that are common elsewhere in North America do not spread far north. Rattlers are among the few that do. They survive the winter by another special adaptation. They have developed the ability to hibernate.

On the prairies of the mid-West and north into Canada, they choose to do so in the burrows of prairie dogs, rodents related to marmots. Elsewhere in the woodlands, they find outcrops of rocks that are riven by deep clefts. But such places are not abundant. As autumn approaches and temperatures fall, great numbers of rattlesnakes set out on long cross-country journeys of many miles following traditional routes to the places where they and their parents before them hibernate each year. Some of these wintering dens may contain a thousand individuals. So those human beings who hate snakes and who, in spite of the rattler's sophisticated early warning system, believe that they are a constant and lethal threat, are also able, at this season of the year, to massacre rattlesnakes in thousands.

As a consequence one of the most advanced and wonderfully sophisticated of all snakes – perhaps of all reptiles – is now, in many parts of the territories it once ruled, in real danger of extinction.

6

The Cold-blooded Truth

Another way of life

All amphibians and reptiles have one thing in common. They are known popularly as 'cold-blooded'. That name is certainly justified for the amphibians. The American wood frog *(Rana sylvatica)* which is found as far north as Alaska, spends over five months of the year in a state of suspended animation, crouched beneath stones or in some other hiding place where it may escape the fierce bite of the cold. It can even withstand up to six degrees of frost for several days on end. During this time a third of its body tissues may become frozen solid. But the frog's hold on life is not totally broken. It has a special physiological response to the challenge. It generates an anti-freeze within its tissues so that its vital core remains unfrozen even if the outer part of its body is below zero degrees.

The Siberian salamander *(Hynobias keyserlingii)* is able to survive even lower temperatures. It lives in the tundra well to the north of the Arctic Circle where the ground has a deep layer that is permanently frozen. It breeds during the short Arctic summer which lasts only three to four months. The newly hatched young take refuge in tussocks of grass and rotten tree roots and there live through the long winter when the temperature falls to minus 15°C. The adults, however, stay closer to the ponds where they bred. There the temperature can drop even farther – to minus 30°C. The advantage of such endurance to them is that when summer at last returns, the first places to thaw are precisely those

near the ponds which are most exposed. So those that hibernate in such positions will be the first to find mates.

But even minus 30°C is within the tolerance of the Siberian salamander. It has survived for several weeks in temperatures of minus 50°C. There was once a suggestion that this astonishing creature could stay alive when frozen for centuries. The story arose because a specimen retrieved from beside the body of a mammoth excavated from the permafrost was still alive when thawed out. It seems, however, that it had not been frozen at the same time as the mammoth but had slipped down a crack in the ground to rest beside the huge prehistoric beast during the previous season.

The common frog *(Rana temporaria)*, Europe's equivalent of America's wood frog, also disappears during the winter. Indeed, it owes its specific name to the fact that its appearance in the countryside is a temporary one. Conrad Gesner who, in the middle of the sixteenth century compiled the first great animal encyclopaedia, called it Ranis temporarius vel aestivus, the temporary or summer frog. Linnaeus, the founder of modern taxonomy, then used the name in a shortened form in his classification. In fact, most common frogs spend the winter close by water or actually in it, buried in the mud at the bottom and extracting what little oxygen they need from the water through their skins. There, provided the water above them is not so shallow that it freezes solid, the lowest temperature they have to endure is, by definition, just above 0°C.

Salamanders as a group positively prefer low body temperatures. The European salamander *(Salamandra salamandra)* is often called a fire salamander because medieval myths maintained that it had the ability to quench fire. How it acquired such a reputation can only be guessed. Perhaps it was because it habitually prefers cold wet places. Wet rotten logs, in which it often conceals itself, might certainly put out a fire. If such a log did so and a salamander subsequently crawled out, the animal might get the blame. The lungless salamanders of North America also actively seek out cool places during the summer to avoid the warmth that could lead to a loss of valuable moisture from their skin. In fact, no amphibian – of any kind or anywhere – has the ability to generate heat within its body as mammals and birds do.

◇

Reptiles, on the other hand can be very warm-blooded indeed. In fact some species may occasionally have blood that is even warmer than our own. There is, nonetheless, a fundamental difference between a reptile's body heat and that of a mammal such as ourselves. Mammals generate their own warmth internally whereas reptiles mainly absorb it from their surroundings. So rather than define animals by the actual temperature of their blood, it is more accurate and informative to call mammals endotherms (animals that gain their warmth from within) and amphibians and reptiles ectotherms (animals that do so from without).

But whereas absorbing heat from the environment is largely a passive process for amphibians, it is not so for reptiles. They have developed behavioural ways of quickly raising the temperature of their bodies and of maintaining it close to their preferred level.

Heat collection begins with the rise of the sun in the morning. Tortoises extend their legs after a night's dormancy, plod out into the open and angle their bodies to catch the first rays. Sometimes they tilt themselves by leaning against a rock in order expose the maximum area of their shells to the sunshine. Some lizards climb into bushes so that they can do so even before the sun's rays strike the ground. Rock absorbs heat, so lizards when they sit on it press their bodies flat against it, drawing their ribs forwards and out-wards. Some chameleons, agamas and geckos turn black for that colour absorbs heat more swiftly than a light one. Later during the day, when there is a risk of over-heating, they do the reverse and become pale or even lemon coloured.

But collecting heat from the sun in this way can be a dangerous process for it requires a reptile to come out of hiding and expose itself in a manner that is bound to attract the attention of predators

A South African armadillo lizard bites its tail in alarm. In such a posture, it convinces most predatory birds that it is uneatable.
▽

such as hawks. One way to minimise that risk is to bask commu-
nally. If there are sunbathers on either side of you, your chances of
being pounced upon are lower than if you are lying stretched out
by yourself. Armadillo lizards *(Cordylus cataphractus)* in South
Africa regularly sunbathe on rocks in rows. They also have a special way of defending themselves. Their bodies are covered with
long sharp and robust spines. If alarmed, they immediately turn
and grip their tails with their mouths in such a way that there is no
free end for a hawk to grasp – only a bundle of very sharp spikes.

The morning, of course, is the time when a reptile is particularly vulnerable for since its body is still comparatively cold it
cannot summon up the energy required to sprint to safety. The
zebra-tailed lizard *(Callisaurus draconoides)* has an ingenious technique of reducing this problem. It buries itself in the desert sand
leaving only its head exposed. This has abundant capillaries
directly beneath the skin. The blood in them absorbs heat and

△
*The zebra-tailed
lizard does not
emerge from beneath
the sand until it has
thoroughly warmed
itself and then, by
waving its tail, it
declares to possible
aggressors that it can
now run so swiftly
that it is not worth
chasing.*

▷
*A horned lizard
responds to threat by
squirting a jet of
blood from its tear
duct.*

258

transports it to the rest of the body underground so that soon the lizard is thoroughly warmed. Only then does it climb out of the sand and start hunting insects.

The horned lizard (*Phrynosoma coronatum*) has elaborated this technique. It has valves in the blood vessels of its head which it can close at will. In the morning, as it lies buried with its head exposed, it shuts them so that blood pools in a cavity around its eye. This warms in the morning sun until it is as much as 5° C above that in the rest of its body. It then can open the valves to allow the warm blood to circulate. But it has also found a second-ary use for this mechanism. If a predator starts to interfere with it, the lizard can squirt this warm blood from its tear duct at its molester. The spray in a thin jet can travel as much as 2 metres (6 feet). It last about a second but can be repeated several times. The lizard rarely does this when human beings pick it up, but fre-quently does so if their attacker is a domestic dog or a coyote. Coyotes are so put out by this that they will drop the lizard. This may be because horned lizards eat ants and the blood may contain

Blood stains the head of a horned lizard after its use in defence.
▽

a substance derived from their formic acid which they find particularly unpleasant.

Good basking sites are vigorously contested. Side-blotched lizards *(Uta stansburiana)* live on open hillsides in California. Most of the slopes are covered by long grass but there are occasional rocky outcrops here and there and it is on these that the lizards do their sun-bathing. The best sites are those that not only have a reasonable expanse of smooth open rock which will absorb the sun's heat but also have boulders on them. These provide elevated sun-bathing platforms which catch the sun first and remain illuminated close to sunset. And even when the sun no longer strikes them, the biggest boulders retain their heat for some time so that the females, flattened against the surface, can still absorb warmth. Boulders also provide other facilities for a lizard. They usually have crevices beneath them where a lizard can take refuge if predators appear, where it can shelter at mid-day if the sun becomes too hot, and where a female can safely leave her eggs. Here, the temperature remains at a pleasant 26–30°C all day long. The males compete vigorously for such boulder-garnished outcrops, chasing one another and defending territory gained by energetically bobbing their heads.

When the time comes for females to copulate and lay, most will visit one of these prime sites and the dominant male who holds it. But which is more important to the female – to secure a vigorous dominant male as the father for their offspring, or to have a good basking rock and a safe place for the eggs? The question is easily answered. Remove some of the crucial boulders from the territory of a dominant male and put them on an outcrop that hitherto had no safe hiding place, no crevice for eggs, and no high basking platform. The male who sits on such a poor site will be low down in the ranking. Within two or three days, he who until then had been largely ignored finds himself being visited by a series of eager females, while the once dominant male, having lost his desirable boulders, is left alone.

◇

The need to control the gain or the loss of body heat imposes a very strict daily routine on many ectotherms. In the Galapagos, marine iguanas *(Amblyrhynchus cristatus)* have a particularly complex and demanding schedule. They live beside the sea on the congealed flows of black basaltic lava that fringe many of the islands. They themselves are as black as the rock on which they lie. Darwin called them 'imps of darkness'. Their dark colour in itself enables them to absorb quickly the maximum amount of heat from the sun's rays.

They spend their nights clumped together or sheltering in the cracks in the lava rocks for although the Galapagos archipelago lies almost exactly on the equator, the nights can be cold and the iguanas need to retain as much as they can of their body heat. As the first rays of the morning sun strike the lava, the iguanas begin to emerge. They move slowly for they do not have energy to spare. Nonetheless, this is a dangerous time. The iguanas are preyed

△
In the morning, Galapagos marine iguanas warm themselves by lying broadside to the rising sun.

upon by Galapagos hawks. The birds, being endotherms, have bodies that are always at the proper working temperature so even in the chill of the morning they can pounce and strike at full speed.

At first the iguanas are cautious and stay close to their crevices. But as the rock warms so more and more of them venture out. The herds thicken and that gives individuals both safety and encouragement. They lie with their flanks turned to the sunshine to heat themselves up as quickly as possible and before long their bodies have warmed to 37°C, their optimum operating temperature. That, as it happens, is ours as well.

The iguanas feed almost entirely on marine algae. If the tide is high, they may have to wait some time before that food is available. But as the water retreats and the weed is exposed, they move down to the sea's edge and begin to graze. Females and young paddle around in the inter-tidal zone, scraping off the algae with the teeth on the side of their jaws. Males, however, are bigger and stronger. They swim out through the breakers, propelling themselves with their undulating tails. And then they dive.

The bigger male marine iguanas have the strength to dive to the sea floor and cling to rocks in order to graze on marine algae.
▽

The algae growing on the sea floor, some 5 metres (15 feet) down is more abundant than it is closer to the shore where all can graze on it, so it well merits the energy spent in reaching it. The males have particularly long claws that enable them to cling to the rock as they feed. But the sea here, in spite of being on the equator, is kept cold – about 15-16°C – by a current that flows up from the far south. The iguanas are able to reduce the heat they lose to the surrounding water by shutting down the blood supply to the outer parts of their body. Even so, their temperature overall drops by some ten degrees. Such a large fall would be lethal for a mammal, but it does not damage the ectothermic iguanas whose body temperatures are continually changing.

They normally feed in water a few metres deep and remain below for no more than five or ten minutes. Exceptionally big males have been recorded as descending to 12 metres (39 feet) and staying there for up to an hour. Darwin recorded some evidence on this point. One of the crew of his ship, the *Beagle*, rather unfeelingly 'sank one with a heavy weight attached to it, thinking

After an exhausting swim during which they lost much of their heat, marine iguanas spreadeagle themselves to warm up in the sun as quickly as possible.
▽

thus to kill it directly; but when, an hour afterwards, he drew up the line, it was quite active'.

Once back on the rocks the iguanas spreadeagle themselves to soak up as much of the sun's heat as quickly as possible. But before long they are in danger of overheating. The temperature on the rocks rises to 50°C and the basalt becomes so hot that it is painful for a human hand to touch. The iguanas now change their orientation. Instead of presenting their flanks to the sun they directly face it, thus substantially reducing the amount of sunshine falling on them. They also straighten their legs and raise their chests so that such cooling breezes as there are may blow beneath them. According to the state of the tides, they may feed again in the afternoon but as the sun sinks, they make their way back into the rocks, there to conserve their heat during the coldness of the night.

◇

The sun, of course, does not shine with equal strength all over the planet. The farther from the equator you travel, the weaker its rays become and the more difficult it is for a reptile to gather all the heat it needs throughout the year.

If reptile eggs get too cold, the embryos within them will die. Most lizards lay their eggs in crevices or bury them in earth or sand and then rely on the sun's heat to help them develop. Reptilian parents, of course, cannot themselves provide the heat for their development in the way that a warm-blooded bird does when it incubates. This factor in itself imposes a northern limit on a reptile's range.

There are some 250 species of lizard belonging to the Lacerta super-family. They are the ones you are most likely to see in Africa and Europe, skittering over rocks, racing through the leaf litter and sunning themselves wherever they find a patch of sunshine. All of them bury their eggs in the ground and then abandon them – all that is except for the most widespread of them, the common European lizard, a little brown reptile, with dark stripes running longitudinally down its body and spotted with yellow or a darker brown. In the Pyrenees, down in the southern part of the species' range, some populations lay eggs like all the rest of the family, but farther north the female retains the fertilised eggs within her body while they develop. By doing this she is able to keep them just as warm as she keeps herself, by moving into whatever patch of sun she can find. After three months, the young finally emerge, each wrapped in a membrane which it breaks by a thrust of its snout. By caring for its eggs in this way, the species has been able to extend its territory right up to the Arctic Circle both in Scandinavia and Siberia.

Animals that give birth to live young are called viviparous. The common European lizard is therefore called, aptly, *Lacerta vivipara*. One species of skink is known to feed its developing young in a somewhat similar way to that used by mammals. They become implanted in the wall of the oviduct. But in most species of viviparous lizards, including *L. vivipara*, the embryo is nourished entirely by the yolk that its mother deposited initially within the egg. Since within the oviduct the shell of an egg has no protective function, it is not hardened with lime but reduced to a thin translucent membrane. However, there is not room in the female's oviduct for as many eggs as she might otherwise produce and lay over a period of several days. *L. vivipara* only produces about half a dozen young whereas other (admittedly bigger) *Lacerta* species may produce several times that number of eggs.

Viviparity is used by many different reptiles to help them extend their range into colder regions. Most geckos lay hard-shelled eggs which they stick to walls or in holes. New Zealand, where winters can be very cold, has 29 species and they, unlike any other geckos in the world, are all viviparous. Chameleons bury their eggs in the ground, except for the viviparous few that live at chilly altitudes in mountains. Two of Britain's native snakes, the grass snake *(Natrix natrix)* and the smooth snake *(Coronella austriaca)* lay eggs. But only the third species, the adder *(Vipera berus)* manages to survive as far north as Scotland – for it is viviparous.

The adder lives even farther north elsewhere – in Finland and

△
A female rattlesnake observes the arrival of her own living young.

Sweden. Here, however, it faces another problem of living in higher latitudes. The summer is very short. Indeed it is so brief that there is not enough time for a female adder to complete her full reproductive cycle. So she starts to produce the eggs in her ovaries not in spring but at the end of the summer. She retains them there throughout the winter and only in the spring of the following year do they complete their development and move down into her oviduct ready for fertilisation by a male. The young are then born – shell-less, needless to say – at the beginning of summer. But the price of doing this and living so far north is that she can only breed once every two years.

Rattlesnakes have universally adopted ovoviviparity. There are over thirty different species of them as well as numerous subspecies. They are found from the jungles of central America, across the United States to the Canadian border and beyond. Brood sizes vary with species. The Mexican species may produce a two dozen

267

or more at one time. In Florida half that number is typical and in
the prairies of the American west broods are even smaller. Farther
north, the broods are smaller still and a female may only be able to
produce young once in two years. But all rattlesnakes give birth to
live young.

◇

No reptile can remain active through the sub-zero temperatures
of a northern winter. They have to take avoiding action. They
hibernate. The process, however, is not so radical as it is for an
endothermic mammal such as, for example, a hedgehog. Mammalian bodily functions have been kept running at a temperature that
has remained constant within a degree or so night and day, spring,
summer and autumn. Switching its organs off is therefore quite a
complex process. Ectotherms on the other hand are accustomed
to great thermal variation within every twenty four hours, so
when they retire to their winter refuge, their bodies simply cool a
little bit further and for a much longer time. They do, however,

*Garter snakes lying
in piles in their
underground winter
refuge.*
▽

Male garter snakes emerge together in spring to await the appearance of the females.

fall very low indeed, to a level where the essential life-sustaining processes are only just ticking over.

The red-sided garter snake *(Thamnophis sirtalis parietalis)* is the most northerly-living of all North American snakes. In western Canada, the temperature in winter can drop to minus 40° C. In the autumn, the garter snakes begin to migrate, travelling some-times for many miles in a purposeful way to outcrops of limestone that are riddled with crevices and sink-holes. The snakes slither inside and assemble in underground chambers. A single one may eventually contain ten thousand of them. There throughout the winter months they lie in great piles, strewn across the rocky floor of the refuge, almost motionless and as cold as the rock beneath them.

In late spring, the temperature begins to rise. When it reaches 25°C, the snakes begin to stir. Suddenly, there is a surge of activity and a great slithering tide erupts from the rocks. But the snakes do not go far. Even though they have starved for so long, they do not

set off to hunt. These first-comers are all males – and they are awaiting the females.

The females soon appear. Unlike the males, they come singly or in small groups. They are many times bigger than the males. Almost immediately each is surrounded by writhing males, all desperate to copulate. To do that, one of them must align his body with that of the female. But this is not easy with so many competitors trying to push him out of the way. Soon each female is enveloped by a tangled ball of males. Eventually one manages to position himself so that his cloaca is in contact with that of the female. Waves of muscular contractions run up and down his body and he manages to insert his penis. The small hooks at its base engage with the scales around the female's cloaca so that even if the female starts to wriggle away he is dragged along with her. The female now releases a pheromone that makes her unattractive to other males. The mating ball quickly unravels, but the

△
A female garter snake, many times the size of a male, is surrounded by a scrum of potential mates, each striving to be the one to fertilise her eggs

copulating pair remain united for a quarter of an hour or so.

Having completed the transfer of sperm, the male then ejects a small gelatinous plug into the female's cloaca and disengages himself. The plug not only makes copulating with a second male physically impossible, it also dissuades other males from even attempting to do so for it contains another pheromone which all males find repugnant. So the unlucky males disperse to try their luck elsewhere and the female, having separated from her mate, sets off on the long journey back to the territory where she lived and hunted the previous year.

The emergence from the cave may continue for several days, sometimes even, sporadically, for weeks. Eventually the garter snakes, in their thousands, are widely distributed once more over the Canadian landscape. As autumn starts to chill into winter, the females give birth. As one might expect for such a northerly reptile, the females are ovoviviparous. Some produce as many as thirty young. Where these go in their first year is not known, but the females then start on their long journey back to their traditional caves. By October they have all, male and female, disappeared into the rocky subterranean chambers where they spend eight months of every year of their adult lives asleep.

◇

No active living reptile has colder blood than the tuatara *(Sphenondon punctata)*. This lizard-like creature looks, superficially at least, somewhat like a small Galapagos marine iguana with a disproportionately large head. Its general body shape is very similar. It has a low crest that runs from its neck down its back along its spine. And it lives on small islands – not, it is true, tropical ones like the roasting Galapagos, but chilly windswept islets off the North Island of New Zealand and in the Cook Strait. During the summer, the islets can be pleasantly warm and the tuatara's body temperature may rise as high as 28°C. But it seldom basks in this warmth. Instead, it lives in burrows and it is only really active at night when it emerges to hunt for insects, snails, worms and sometimes the chicks of seabirds.

The tuatara's most efficient operating temperature seems to be around 12° C. At such low temperatures, the chemistry of an animal's body works very slowly indeed and in consequence, the tuatara has a very lethargic life style. It only breathes about once every seven seconds, even when active, and when resting it may go for an hour without breathing at all. It takes about twenty years to grow to maturity. A female, having started to develop her eggs within her oviduct, needs four years to complete them. Even wrapping a shell around them, which a bird manages in a matter of a few hours, takes her six to eight months. And once her eggs have been laid, they take about fourteen months to hatch – the longest embryonic development of any reptile. Such is life in the slow lane. On the other hand, it is thought that tuataras may live for as much as a hundred and twenty years or more – and that is longer than any known lizard.

△
The New Zealand tuatara, whose blood is so cold that it lives at an extremely slow pace.

But though the tuatara looks like a lizard and was indeed initially classified as one when it was first discovered by European scientists in the nineteenth century, it is anatomically very different indeed. The male has no organ for inserting his sperm into the body of the female, as tortoises and crocodiles, lizards and snakes have. A pair copulate by simply pressing their two cloacas together. The vertebrae in a tuatara's spine are not connected by ball and socket joints as they are in all modern lizards (except most geckos) but by a binding of fibrous tissue. It has an extra vertebra between its first so-called 'atlas' vertebra and the skull itself. It lacks an external ear. And whereas modern lizards have only one window-like gap in the side of their skull, the tuatara has two, one above the other.

Fossils virtually identical to the tuatara have been found in two hundred million year old Late Triassic rocks. It is one of the most primitive of living reptiles. At one time, some suggested that it was closely related to the dinosaurs, but that is not thought to be the case. It belongs to the same broad group as lizards and snakes and its low temperature life-style is not necessarily a primitive condition. Nonetheless it prompts speculations as to whether the dinosaurs themselves were ectothermic or endothermic.

◇

There is some evidence that suggests that at least some prehistoric giant reptiles collected energy direct from the sun. *Dimetrodon* looked rather like a huge three-metre-long monitor lizard except for the fact that it carried on its back a semi-circular fan of skin, supported by elongated spines growing from each vertebra. If the skin covering this fan contained abundant capillaries (and there are some signs that it did) then when the animal lay broadside to the sun the fan could have served as a solar panel, gathering heat. Conversely, if the animal faced the sun at mid-day, the fan could equally well have acted as a radiator, dispersing unwanted and possibly dangerous heat. It is difficult to imagine what other function this large structure might have had, except perhaps the even more unlikely one of serving as some kind of display. *Dimetrodon*,

however, belonged to the reptile group which ultimately gave rise to the mammals, and was not a dinosaur.

Stegosaurus, on the other hand, was indeed a dinosaur and one that weighed some four tonnes and grew to a length of 8 metres (26 feet). It had two lines of triangular plates, one either side of the backbone that extended from the back of its neck to the end of its tail. At either end the plates were comparatively small but they increased in size towards the middle. Above the hips they were some two metres in height. Initially, palaeontologists thought these plates had a defensive function – even though they would have failed to give any protection to the stegosaur's broad flanks. Then it was noticed that their surface is covered with a tangle of wandering grooves. These seem to be marks left by capillaries, and when the plates were sectioned they were found to have a spongy structure suggesting that in life they had contained a great deal of blood. Experiments were carried with models of the plates in wind tunnels and they demonstrated that the triangular shape of the plates was ideal for dispersing heat. So it seems that *Stegosaurus* used its back plates as radiators and doubtless as solar panels too.

△
The fossil of a Stegosaurus complete with the plates that fringed its back and may have had a thermal function.

Such huge and elaborate devices for heat-exchange imply that stegosaurs were partly if not entirely ectothermic. But this family is one of the earlier groups of dinosaurs. What about the biggest and most celebrated species, the terrifying *Tyrannosaurus* and the monstrous sauropods of the Cretaceous period that weighed thirty tonnes or more and measured 40 metres (130 feet).

Evidence comes from several sources. First, the bones. An ectothermic animal will grow faster during the summer than the winter. Bone that is produced during rapid growth tends to be rather more spongy than that which is laid down more slowly. Variations in seasonal growth could therefore produce a series of concentric rings in a leg bone rather like the concentric rings in the trunk of a tree. This can indeed be seen in living ectothermic reptiles. Such bones of large dinosaurs as have been investigated do not seem to show such rings. Consequently, one might conclude that these animals had grown at a steady rate, winter and summer, and that therefore they must have been indeed endothermic. However, to make the argument really convincing, the comparison should be made between similar-sized animals – and there is no living ectotherm the size of a giant dinosaur.

Secondly, a clue might come from the relative numbers of carnivorous and herbivorous dinosaurs. An endothermic hunter, such as a lion, requires much more food than an ectothermic hunter of equivalent size and weight, such as a crocodile. Some calculations suggest that the endotherm must consume ten times as much. So if there are very few carnivorous dinosaurs compared with herbivorous ones in a given eco-system, then this will indicate that they were indeed endothermic.

The problem with this argument is that the fossil record is selective and patchy, as is recognised by all palaeontologists. Different animals, living in different ways in different niches, will have different chances of being fossilised, so we cannot presume that the proportion of preserved bones exactly mirrors the proportion of different species alive at any one time. This is thought by many to disqualify the evidence, no matter what the relative numbers of fossils of each kind there may be in museum collections.

Thirdly, there is the evidence of dinosaur behaviour as revealed by their tracks. Single footprints of dinosaurs are not uncommon. From such spoor we may be able to deduce the weight of an animal. In some remarkable sites there are continuous trails containing many prints. If we can be sure of the identity of the printmaker, and therefore know its limb length from its fossilised skeleton, the spacing of such prints will indicate the speed at which it was travelling. Such evidence supports the idea that some dinosaurs, particularly the small ones that stood on two legs like flightless birds, were indeed capable of considerable speeds. But then some large ectotherms today like crocodiles and goannas can also run very fast.

In a few rare and exciting sites there are abundant prints and long trails made by different sized animals. These can be even more revealing. Such a place is Purgatoire Creek in a remote part of south-eastern Colorado in the American west. Reaching it is

△

The placing of footprints, like these of sauropod dinosaurs in Purgatoire Creek, Colorado, can reveal a great deal about the habits, and even the blood temperatures, of the creatures that made them.

not easy and involves a five-mile hike but once there, the tracks are spectacular. They were imprinted in soft mud at the edge of a freshwater lake. Today the mud has become a sandy limestone. In one part of the valley, the river has eroded it away, layer by layer. At least three of the layers contain tracks. Some were made by small theropod dinosaurs, three-toed carnivorous creatures that walked on their hind legs. Others, larger, more rounded and deeper, were left by brontosaurs, much bigger herbivorous dinosaurs that stood some five metres high at the shoulder and weighed 33 tonnes or more. These prints are almost a metre across. In one place there are trails left by about a hundred individuals that extend for some 400 metres. In places where a branch of the river covers them with shallow rippling water, it is very easy indeed to imagine that the prints are not in rock but were made only a few hours previously in what is still soft mud – and to glance uneasily over your shoulder.

Such sites as these can be very informative to anyone who has experience of tracking living animals in the wilderness today. They reveal that some dinosaurs travelled in herds of some considerable size and that these were often composed of different sized individuals, suggesting that juveniles formed the core of the herd and adults travelled protectively around the edges. Animals living in groups with a complex social structure such as this, so the argument goes, must have had quite an advanced brain like a mammal's, which would require a constant body temperature. No ectotherm today lives in such structured communities.

Perhaps the most convincing evidence for endothermy comes from the theropod dinosaurs. This is the group that is most closely related to birds. Among them are not only the gigantic *Tyrannosaurus* which may well have been a scavenger but also small hyper-active hunters like *Velociraptor* and *Deinonychus* that stood on their hind legs and were capable of running at great speed. Like most dinosaurs they had large brains. But large brains do not function properly if they are allowed to cool down and warm up every twenty-four hours.

Small species from this group discovered recently in China

clinch the argument. Small bodies lose heat more quickly than warm bodies, so insulation of some kind would have been of particular importance to such species. And the Chinese theropods, marvellously preserved, show conclusively that their bodies were covered with feathers. There is no evidence that these creatures were able to fly. Their feathery coating was an insulator to help them retain their expensive internally-generated heat. Only later were they used as aerofoils when the theropods' warm-blooded descendants, the birds, finally took to the air.

But even if dinosaurs were not able to generate their own heat, the bigger species must nonetheless have been warm-blooded. We know from tracks that even the giant species moved at considerable speeds and to generate the energy necessary to do that, their body temperature must have been quite high. If they had warm blood at any time, they must have had it for most of the time. For just as a small body loses heat quickly, so a large one retains it for a long time. So a twenty-ton dinosaur that had a body warm enough to enable it to run during the day would not lose very much of its heat during a single night before it was able to raise it again to optimum levels in the morning sun.

◇

A few reptiles alive today are also warm-blooded largely because of their great size. The biggest of the turtles, the giant leatherback is one such. It can weigh half a tonne and be two metres long. Simply contracting a muscle generates heat. We ourselves use the method in an emergency when a cold environment threatens to chill us faster than we can generate internal heat in a normal way. So we shiver – and the rapid contraction of our muscles warms us. Thus the mere act of swimming warms the body of the leatherback. Its body is swathed by a thick layer of fat which acts as a very effective heat insulator and its great size further reduces the loss of any heat that might escape through the fat. So the leatherback's internal temperature is significantly above that of the water that surrounds it. This enables it to extend its range well beyond the tropics, down to the far south around New Zealand, north to the coast of Britain and even beyond to Norway and Iceland and the ice pack off Newfoundland. It also enables it to dive to great depths without being unduly affected by the low temperatures found in such regions.

Other reptiles also actively use muscular effort to generate heat. Several species of python, including the African rock python *(Python sebae)* and the reticulated python *(Python reticulatus)*, unusually for reptiles, stay with their eggs, guarding them against predators such as monitor lizards. Asian pythons *(Python molurus)* and some Australian ones live in regions that are cooler than equatorial Africa and not only guard their eggs but actively incubate them. The female diamond python *(Morelia spilota)* wraps her coils around her clutch of a dozen or so and stays with it for up to a hundred days. For long periods during this time she will contract her body spasmodically, about thirty times a minute. By doing this she generates enough heat to keep her eggs at a temperature of about 25°C. That is often 9° above her surroundings during the day and as much as 18° at night. Doing this, of course, takes

A female python curls herself around her clutch of eggs, not only guarding them but actively warming them by twitching her muscles.

▽

energy and since she does not feed at all during incubation, a female may lose as much as 15% of her body weight before her eggs hatch.

◇

Endothermy brings great benefits. It enables an animal to be ready for immediate action – whether to pounce or to flee – at any time, in the cool of the night or the heat of the day. It also allows its practitioners to colonise regions where an ectotherm would be frozen solid throughout the year. Generating heat internally also enables an animal to keep the temperature of its body constant to within a degree or so. That in turn makes it possible to operate structures and mechanisms that can undertake complex physio-logical tasks that are not possible in other circumstances. In particular it permits the development and functioning of a brain capable of processing multiple stimuli and issuing immediate con-sequential commands.

But endothermy is also very expensive. Stoking the internal fires and keeping them burning continuously consumes a great deal of fuel. Eighty per cent of all the food a human being eats is used for this one purpose. To ingest sufficient for its needs a rabbit has to spend many hours of both the day and the night nibbling grass. It even eats its own faeces to extract the last few calories of nourishment. A marine iguana in the Galapagos, on the other hand, since it collects its body heat directly from the sun, can thrive by doing no more than scrape seaweed for an hour or so from rocks at low tide. A polar bear, well furred and insulated from the cold, can generate enough bodily heat to enable it to remain active in the Arctic. But in order to do that it is compelled to hunt every two or three days. If it cannot find enough food then the Arctic is as uninhabitable for it as it is for a reptile.

The tropical rain forest is the richest and most beneficent of all earthly environments. Here there is a superabundance of food for all its inhabitants. But even so, a mammalian hunter needs to kill very frequently if it is to keep its body functioning properly. A leopard needs to eat food of some kind every two or three days if it is to remain in good condition. A five metre long python, with a body of around the same weight, needs only one large meal a year.

In the deserts of the world, life is very hard indeed for a mammal. Food is very scarce. So is water and a mammal needs water if only to cool itself, either by panting or by sweating. Hunting has to be restricted to the colder nights and even then prey is desperately rare. By contrast, deserts suit a reptile very well indeed. The sun supplies it with all the energy it needs to be active and there is enough food in the shape of insects, scorpions or other smaller reptiles to satisfy its modest needs.

Today, the earth's climate is changing. The frigid frontier that kept reptiles out of the Arctic is now advancing towards the Pole. The permafrost that stunted growth on the tundra is beginning to melt and the coniferous forest is creeping northwards. In the south, the great ice shelves that fringed Antarctica are breaking up and drifting away. It may not be long before the bare rocky edge of the entire continent reappears. In more temperate regions, woodlands and rain forests are dwindling and deserts are spreading. Mammals everywhere are finding it increasingly hard to collect all the food they require.

But the reptiles, the first large animals to colonise the dry land, being so efficient and economic in their exploitation of the sources of energy needed to do so, seem likely to be extending their empires in the world that is coming. Sixty-five million years ago they suffered a great catastrophe. But – whatever it was – it did not exterminate them all. Their day is certainly not yet over.

Acknowledgments

Herpetologists – those who study amphibians and reptiles – seem to have a particularly intense enthusiasm for their subject. Perhaps it is the fact that many such creatures are so utterly different from mammals in both their look and their behaviour that makes them particularly interesting and attractive. Whatever the reason, I soon discovered when writing this book and working on the films that were being made at the same time, that no matter what species I was concerned with, there was a herpetologist who was devoted to it, who knew not only exactly where it could be found but precisely when it would behave in the way that particularly interested us.

I am thus greatly indebted to herpetologists around the world who not only introduced me to a particular species but who guided my eye in seeing details that might have otherwise escaped me and who, after long hot days spent in the field watching and filming, spent their evenings in happy conversation, discussing and analysing what we had seen.

Among those to whom I am particularly grateful are: in Australia, Warrick Angus, Peter Bartlett, Adam Britton, Steven Brooks, Mike Bull, Brian Bush, Chris Clemente and Aaron Fenner; in Britain, Nick Arnold and David Norman; in the Galapagos, Felipe Cruz; in Madagascar, Bertrand Razafimahatratra; in Menorca, Valentin Perez Mellado; in Panama, Erik Lindquist, Edgardo Griffiths and Karel Warkentin; in Singapore, James Gan and Siva Sivasotho; in South Africa, Donald Strydom, Sean Thomas and Martin Whiting; in the United States, Fred Antonio, Ray Ashton, Kathy Bishop, Roulon Clarke, Harry Greene, Martin Lockley, Wade Sherbrooke, Barry Sinervo and Stan Trauth.

I have a particular debt to Nick Arnold who, mercifully, read the whole text and steered me away from error.

Herpetologists are not only academics. Some, fortunately for me, are also television directors and several worked on the films that accompany this book. My gratitude certainly goes to them in particular, but I am also indebted to the rest of the production team. They all, one way or another, contributed to this book. Their names are listed opposite.

LIFE IN COLD BLOOD

The Television Team

Series Producer
Miles Barton

Executive Producer
Sara Ford

Senior Producer
Hilary Jeffkins

Producers
James Brickell
Adam White

Director
Scott Alexander

Researchers
Nikki Stew
Paul Williams

Production Co-ordinators
Jenni Collie
Esther O'Donnell
Alison Ritchie

Production Team Assistant
Sam Taylor

Production Manager
Ruth Flowers
Lynn Barry

Music
David Poore
Ben Salisbury

Graphic Design
Mick Connaire

Sound Recordists
Warwick Finlay
Chris Watson

Film Editing
Andrew Chastney
Tim Coope
Andrew Mort
Dave Pearce

Dubbing Editors
Paul Cowgill
Paul Fisher
Angela Groves
Kate Hopkins

Dubbing Mixers
Peter Davies
Martyn Harries
Stephen Williams

Colourists
Jonathon Prosser
Luke Rainey

Photography
Luke Barnett
Keith Brust
Rod Clarke
Richard Fitzpatrick
Kevin Flay
Mark Lamble
Alastair MacEwen
Mark MacEwen
Michael Male
Justin Maguire
Peter Nearhos
Paul Stewart
Gavin Thurston
David Wright
Mark Yates

3D Animation
Jeremy Horton
Moving Picture
Company

◇

Series scientific consultant
Tim Halliday

Sources of Photographs

Frontispiece Nick Garbutt (NPL)

8 Stephen Dalton (NHPA)

11 Ted Deschler (VIREO)

13 ANT Photo Library (NHPA)

14 Michael Dick (OSF)

15 Daniel Heuclin (NHPA)

16 Oxford Scientific Films (OSF)

17 Bruno Pambour (BIOS)

19 David Kjaer (NPL)

20 Oxford Scientific Films (OSF)

21 Michel Rauch (BIOS)

22 David Dennis (OSF)

23 Raymond Mendez (OSF)

24 Stan Trauth

25 Stan Trauth

27 Oxford Scientific Films (OSF)

29 Alastair Macewen

31 Daniel Heuclin (BIOS)

33 Stephen Dalton (NHPA)

34 *above:* Konrad Wothe (OSF)

34 *below:* Michael Fogden (OSF)

36 *above:* Michael & Patricia Fogden (Minden Pictures/FLPA)

36 *below:* Paul Franklin (OSF)

37 Miles Barton

38 Anthony Bannister (NHPA)

40 **a**: Paul Franklin (OSF)

40 **b**: Denis Bringard (BIOS)

40 **c**: Nigel Cattlin (FLPA)

40 **d**: Jane Burton (NPL)

40 **e**: Oxford Scientific Films (OSF)

40 **f**: Oxford Scientific Films (OSF)

40 **g**: George Bernard (NHPA)

40 **h**: Jef Meul (Photo Natura/FLPA)

43 Oxford Scientific Films (OSF)

44 Michael & Patricia Fogden (Minden Pictures/FLPA)

46 Pierre Huguet (BIOS)

48 *above:* Sauvanet Jany (BIOS)

48 *below:* Daniel Heuclin (BIOS)

50 Mark Payne-Gill (NPL)

53 James Carmichael Jr (NHPA)

54 Mark Moffett (Minden Pictures/FLPA)

55 Michael Fogden (OSF)

56 Michael Fogden (OSF)

57 *above:* Michael & Patricia Fogden (Minden Pictures/FLPA)

57 *below:* Michael & Patricia Fogden (Minden Pictures/FLPA)

59 ANT Photo Library (NHPA)

60 Chris Mattison (FLPA)

62 *above:* Nick Gordon (NPL)

62 *centre:* Paul Freed (OSF)

62 *below:* Pete Oxford (Minden Pictures/FLPA)

63 *above:* Philie Clement (NPL)

63 *centre:* Brian Kenney (OSF)

63 *below:* Luis Casiano (BIOS)

65 Wayne Lawler (Auscape)

70 Erwin and Peggy Bauer (Auscape)

73 *above:* Chris Mattison (FLPA)

73 *below:* Robert Lubeck (Animals Animals)

74 Konrad Wothe (Minden Pictures/FLPA)

75 Brian Kenney (OSF)

76 David Curl (OSF)

78 David Attenborough

82 David Attenborough

85 Mark Jones (OSF)

86 Mark Jones (OSF)

88 Mark Jones (OSF)

89 Frans Lanting (Minden Pictures/FLPA)

91 Jurgen & Christine Sohns (FLPA)

92 Stephen Krasemann (NHPA)

95 Olivier Groenewald (OSF)

97 Mark O'Shea (NHPA)

99 Mark Bowler (NHPA)

101 Norbert Wu (Minden Pictures/FLPA)

102 Doug Perrine (NPL)

104 Doug Perrine (NPL)

106 Michael Patrick O'Neill (NHPA)

107 Kevin Schafer (NHPA)

108 Arnaud Greth (BIOS)

110 B Jones & M Shimlock (NHPA)

112 Michael Patrick O'neill (NHPA)

114 Roger De laHarpe (Animals Animals)

115 ANT Photo Library (NHPA)

116 J & A Scott (NHPA)

120 Tony Heald (NPL)

125 *above:* Fritz Polking (FLPA)

125 *below:* Frans Lanting (Minden Pictures/FLPA)

127 Jany Sauvanet (NHPA)

128 Chris Perrins (OSF)

130 Steven David Miller (NPL)

131 Adrian Warren (Ardea)

132 Michael & Patricia Fogden (Minden Pictures/FLPA)

133 Adrian Warren (Ardea)

134 Mark Deeble & Victoria Stone (OSF)

136 Sylvain Cordier (BIOS)

138 Anup Shah (NPL)

139 Mark Deeble & Victoria Stone (OSF)

140 Gabriel Rojo (NPL)

142 Jean-Claude Carton (BIOS)

144 Joe McDonald (OSF)

147 *above:* Martin Wendler (NHPA)

147 *below:* Solvin Zankl (NPL)

148 *above:* Michael D. Kern (NPL)

148 *below:* Brandon Cole (BIOS)

151 Gerry Ellis (Minden Pictures/FLPA)

152 Luis Casiano (BIOS)

154 Michael & Patricia Fogden (Minden Pictures/FLPA)

155 Stephen Dalton (NHPA)

156 Jean-Paul Ferrero (Auscape)

158 Nick Garbutt (NPL)

159 Ken Preston-Mafham (prema)

160 Harvey Martin (BIOS)

162 Jose B. Ruiz (NPL)

165 Nick Garbutt (NPL)

166 Mark Moffett (Minden Pictures/FLPA)

168 *above:* Daniel Heuclin (NHPA)

168 *below:* Daniel Heuclin (NHPA)

170 Jose B. Ruiz (NPL)

171 Michael & Patricia Fogden (Minden Pictures/FLPA)

172 Pierre Huguet (BIOS)

173 Terry Whittaker (FLPA)

174 Ingo Arndt (Photo Natura/FLPA)

175 Oxford Scientific Films (OSF)

176 Mary McDonald (NPL)

177 Michael & Patricia Fogden (Minden Pictures/FLPA)

178 Nick Garbutt (NPL)

179 Pete Oxford (NPL)

180 Bill Love (NHPA)

182 Oxford Scientific Films (OSF)

184 Michael Pitts (NPL)

186 Michael Pitts (NPL)

188 Edwin Sadd (OSF)

189 Michael Pitts (NPL)

191 *above:* Daniel Heuclin (NHPA)

191 *below:* Mitsuaki Iwago (Minden Pictures/FLPA)

192 Miles Barton

195 Mark O'Shea (NHPA)

196 Daniel Heuclin (NHPA)

198 Tony Phelps (NPL)

199 Mark O'Shea (NHPA)

200 Emile Barbelette (BIOS)

201 Daniel Heuclin (NHPA)

202 Robert Valentic (NPL)

203 Daniel Heuclin (NHPA)

204 Chris Mattison (FLPA)

208 Chris Mattison (FLPA)

211 *above:* Mike Hill (OSF)

211 *below:* Zig Leszczynski (OSF)

213 Austin J Stevens (Animals Animals)

214 Daniel Heuclin (NHPA)

216 Montford Thierry (BIOS)

218 Fritz Polking (FLPA)

221 Montford Thierry (BIOS)

223 Stephen Dalton (NHPA)

224 *above:* Michael & Patricia Fogden (Minden Pictures/FLPA)

224 *below:* Michael & Patricia Fogden (Minden Pictures/FLPA)

226 Daniel Heuclin (NHPA)

227 Mark O'Shea (NHPA)

228 Cede Prudente (NHPA)

229 Anthony Bannister (NHPA)

230 Anthony Bannister (NHPA)

231 Daniel Heuclin (NHPA)

232 Daniel Heuclin (BIOS)

234 Tony Crocetta (BIOS)

235 Anthony Bannister (OSF)

236 *above:* Michael & Patricia Fogden (Minden Pictures/FLPA)

236 *below:* Michael & Patricia Fogden (Minden Pictures/FLPA)

238 Reinhard Dirscherl (BIOS)

241 Anthony Bannister (NHPA)

242 Joe McDonald (OSF)

244 *above:* Austin J Stevens (Animals Animals)

244 *below:* Chris Mattison (FLPA)

247 Zig Leszczynski (OSF)

249 Roger de la Harpe (Animals Animals)

250 Joe McDonald (OSF)

255 T Kitchin & V Hurst (NHPA)

257 Daniel Heuclin (BIOS)

258 Michael & Patricia Fogden (Minden Pictures/FLPA)

259 Oxford Scientific Films (OSF)

260 John Cancalosi (NPL)

262 D Parer and E Parer-Cook (Auscape)

263 Tui De Roy (Minden Pictures/FLPA)

264 Nancy Rotenberg (Animals Animals)

267 Daniel Heuclin (BIOS)

268 François Gohier (Ardea)

269 François Gohier (Ardea)

270 David Dennis (OSF)

272 Pete Oxford (NPL)

274 François Gohier (Ardea)

276 Claude Steelman (OSF)

279 Paul Freed (OSF)

Index

This index to animals covered in the book has their common names followed by their scientific names. Page-reference in **bold** type are to illustrations.

COMMON NAMES

adder 266, **266**
adder, puff 245
agama 149, **152**
alligator 124, 128, 134-5, **125, 130**
amphisbaenian 203, 222, **203**
anaconda 220, 222, **221**
anguid 200
anole 153, 165, **154**
arrau 98, **99**
axolotl 15-16, **8, 16**

basilisk 146, **144-5**
blind-snake 208, **208**
boa 210, 215
boa constrictor 221
boa, dwarf 207
boa, emerald tree 212, **211, 216**
boomslang 225, 231
bullfrog, African 49, **50-1**
bullfrog, South American 42
bushmaster 245

caecilian 26-9, **27, 29**
caiman, black 124
caiman, Cuvier's dwarf **127**
chameleon, Jackson's 166
chameleon, Meller's 166
chameleon, panther **158**
chameleon, Parson's **159, 160**
chameleon, pygmy 167, **166**
chameleon, snub-nosed **165**
chi-chak 172-3, **173**
cobra, black-necked 235
cobra, Egyptian 235, **234**
cobra, king 241, **242-3**
cobra, Mozambique 235
cobra, rinkhals 235
cobra, spitting 235, **235**
colubrid 222-3, **229, 231**
colubrid, African 229
crocodile, African dwarf 126
crocodile, American 126
crocodile, Nile 126, 135, **114, 120-1, 133-7, 138-9**

crocodile, saltwater 113-20, **115, 116-7**

diapsid 68
dinosaur, sauropod **276**
dragon, flying 153, **155**
dragon, Komodo 182, **184-5, 186**

elapid 233, 237
emydid 91
eusuchian 123

fer-de-lance 245
frog, African tree 43, **44-5**
frog, American wood 254, **254**
frog, arrow-poison 53-4, **62-3**
frog, Australian water-holding 64
frog, common European 39, 42, 255, **40, 255**
frog, Darwin's 58, **57**
frog, edible European **34**
frog, gastric brooding 58, **59**
frog, gladiator 49
frog, golden 37, **37**
frog, goliath 30, **31**
frog, hairy 39
frog, kokoi 61
frog, 'flying' **2**, 32
frog, marsupial 55-6, **56**
frog, painted reed 38, **38**
frog, pygmy marsupial **55**
frog, South American tree 49, 52, **34**
frog, tungara **36**
frog, Venezuelan varnishing 60, **60**
frog, Wallace's 'flying' **33**
frog, water-holding 64, **65**
frog, wood **255**

gecko, chi-chak172, **172**
gecko, common Mediterranean 171
gecko, frilled 177 **179**
gecko, Phelsuma **180**
gecko, Turkish **170**
gecko 171, 176, 266, **171, 174-7, 266**

gharial 128, 133, **128-9, 132**
Gila monster 231, **231**
goanna 149

iguana, green146, **142, 147**
iguana, Caribbean 149, **148**
iguana, land, 149snake, yellow-bellied sea 240, **241**
iguana, marine 262-5, **262-4**
iguanian 143, 149
Komodo dragon 182-6, 231, **184-5, 186**
krait 233

lash-tail 149
lizard, alligator 200
lizard, armadillo 257, **258**
lizard, beaded 231, **232**
lizard, blind 201
lizard, common European 265
lizard, flying 153, 225
lizard, frilled 157, **156**
lizard, glass 201
lizard, green 167, **168**
lizard, horned 260, **259, 260**
lizard, Mexican legless 205, **204**
lizard, moloch 150, **151**
lizard, monitor 181, 187, 231, **169, 188**
lizard, side-blotched 261
lizard, sleepy 190
lizard, shingleback 190
lizard, zebra-tailed 258, **258**
lungfish 11-12
lungfish, Queensland 12, **13**

mamba, black 212
mamba, green **226**
mata-mata 95, **95**
mesosuchian 123
monitor, lace 189
monitor, water **182**
mud puppy, 15

newt, great crested 18, **19, 20**

olm, 16-17, **17**

perentie 187

protosuchian 123
pygopodid 203, **202**
python 207, 210, 215, **211,
 218-19**, **279**
python, African rock 221, 279
python, amethystine 221
python, carpet **213**
python, diamond 279
python, green tree 212
python, Indian 221-2
python, reticulated 221-2, 279

rattlesnake, timber 246, **247**
rattlesnake 215, 245, 250, 252,
 267, **214**, **250**, **267**

salamander, European fire 20,
 256. **21**, **256**
salamander, Japanese giant 14,
 14-15
salamander, lungless 23
salamander, mud puppy 15
salamander, olm 16-17, **17**
salamander, Siberian 254
salamander, slimy 24-6, **24-5**
salamander, three-lined **22**
salamander, tree **23**
saltie *see* saltwater crocodile
sea-krait, yellow-lipped **238-9**
sheltopusik 200, **201**
shingleback 190
skink, blind 197-8
skink, blue-tongued 190, **191**
skink, dart 197
skink, keeled 197
skink, legless, **198**
skink, pygmy blue-tongued 194,
 195
skink, sand 197
skink, sandfish **196**
skink, shingleback **192**
skink, Solomon Islands giant 190,
 191
slow-worm, European 199, **200**
snake, Allen's coral 237
snake, bird 225
snake, colubrine 233
snake, coral 237, **236**
snake, crab-eating 225
snake, egg-eating 229-30, **229-30**
snake, European whip 223
snake, flowerpot 209
snake, garter 269-71, **269-71**

snake, grass 223, 266, **223**
snake, king **236**
snake, neck-banded 237
snake, paradise flying 225-9, **227,
 228**
snake, sand 223
snake, sea 240, **238-41**
snake, shovel-nosed 229
snake, smooth 266
snake, tentacled 225, **224**
snake, tree (boomslang) 225, 231
snake, twig 225, **224**
snake. western whip 223
snake, wolf 229
snake, yellow-bellied sea 240, **241**
synapsid 68

tadpole 41-2, 59 **40**
terrapin, Florida red-belly 91-4
 135
terrapin, pond 94
terrapin, red-eared 94, **92-3**
theropod 277
toad, cane 61
toad, midwife 46-7, **46**
toad, square-marked **36**
toad, Surinam 30, 47, **48**
tortoise, angulate 76, **76**
tortoise, Burmese brown 90
tortoise, Galapagos giant 83-9, **84,
 86**, **88**, **89**
tortoise, gopher 74-6, **75**
tortoise, Greek 72, **74**
tortoise, hinged 90
tortoise, North American wood
 88
tortoise, Seychelles giant 79-83,
 82
tuatara 271-3, **272**
Tui Malila, 78, **78**
turtle, alligator snapper **70-1**
turtle, Atlantic ridley **104-5**
turtle, Florida box **73**
turtle, flatback 100
turtle, freshwater **99**
turtle, giant Malaysian soft-shell
 96
turtle, green 100, 111, **110**, **112**
turtle, hawksbill 100, **101**
turtle, leatherback 101, 103-9,
 106, **107**, **108**
turtle, marine 99
turtle, mata-mata95, **95**

turtle, Pacific ridley, 100
turtle, pig-nose 96-7, **97**
turtle, snake-necked 95
turtle, soft-shelled 96

viper, Gaboon 245, **244**, **249**
viper, pit 245, 249, **244**

worm-lizard 205

SCIENTIFIC NAMES

Ablepharus 197
Acontias 197
Alligator mississippiensis 124
Alligator sinensis 128
Alytes obstetricans 46
Amblyrhynchus cristatus 149, 262
Ambystoma mexicanum 15-16, **8,
 16**
Andrias japonicus 14
*Anolis*153
*Archelon*99
Assa darlingtoni 56
Atelopus ziteki 37, **37**

Basiliscus plumifrons 146
Bipes 204
Bitis gabonica 245
Boa constrictor 221
Breviceps adspersus 39
Brookesia minima 167
Bufo marinus 61

Callisaurus draconoides 258
Caretta caretta 100
Carettochelys insculpta 96
Ceratophrys 60
Chameleo jacksoni 166
Chameleo mellen 166
Chameleo oustaleti 166
Chelonia depressa 100
Chelonia mydas 100
Chelonoides carbonaria 88
Chelys fimbriata 95, **95**
Chersina angulata 76, **76**
Chionactis occipitalis 229
Chiromantis 43
Chlamydosaurus kingi 157
Chondropython viridis 212
Chrysopelea paradisi 225, 228,
 226, **228**
Conolophus pallidus 149
Conolophus subcristatus 149

Index

Conraua goliath 30
Corallus canina 212
Cordylus cataphractus 258
Coronella austriaca 266
Corucia zebrata 190
Crocodylus acutus 126
Crocodylus niloticus 126
Crocodylus porosus 113-20, **115,
116-17**
Crotalus cerastes 215
Crotalus horridus 246

Dasypelta scabra 229
Deinonychus 277
Deinosuchus 123
Dendraspis polylepis 212
Dendrobates 52-3, 61-4
Dendrobates auratus **63**
Dendrobates azureus **62**
Dendrobates imitator 53
Dendrobates leucomelas **63**
Dendrobates pumilo **63**
Dendrobates sylvaticus **62**
Dendrobates tinctorius **62**
Dermatochelys coriacea 101
Dibamidae 201
Dimetrodon 273
Dipsochelys dussumieri 81
Dispholidus typus 225
Draco volans 153, 225

Emys orbicularis 94
Eretmochelys imbricata 100, **101**
Erpeton tentaculatus 225
Eunectes murinus 221

Fordonia leucobalia 225

Gastrotheca marsupiata 55
Gastrotheca ovifera 56
Gastrotheca weinlandii 60
Gavialis gangeticus 128
Gekko gecko 172
Geochelone radiata 78
Gopherus polyphemus 74

Heloderma horridum 231
Heloderma suspectum 231
Hemachatus haemachatus 235
Hemidactylus frenatus 172
Hemidactylus turcicus 171
Hierrophis viridiflavus 223

Homeosaurus 273
Hyla faber 49
Hyla rosenbergi 49
Hynobias keyserlingii 254
Hyperolius marmoratus 38, **38**

Ichthyostega 12, 59
Iguana iguana 146

Kinixys homeana 72, 90

Lacerta vivipara 167-71, 265-6
Lepidochelys kempi 100
Lepidochelys oliveacea 100
Lepidosiren paradoxa 12
Leptodactylus pentadactylus 42
Lycodon 229

Mabuya 197
Macroclemys temmincki 69, **70-1**
Manouria emys 90
Megachelys trijuga 94
Melanosuchus niger 124
Micrurus alleni 237
Moloch horridus 150
Morelia spilota 279

Naja mossambica 235
Naja naja 235
Naja nigricollis 235
Natrix natrix 223, 266
Necturus maculosus 15
Neoceratodus forsteri 12
Neoseps 197
Notaden 64, **65**

Ophiophagus hannah 241
Ophisaurus apodus 200
Osteolaemus tetraspis 126

Palaeosuchus palebrosus 126
Paleosuchus trigonatus 126
Pelamis platinus 240
Pelochelys bibroni 96
Phelsuma 178, **180**
Phrynosoma coronatum 260
Phyllobates bicolor 61
Phyllomedusa sauvagei 60, **60**
Pipa pipa 30, 47, **48**
Plethodon albagula 24
Podocnemis unifilis 98
Proteus anguineus 16, **17**
Protopterus 12

Psammophis leightoni 223
Pseudemys nelsoni 135
Pseustes 225
Ptenopus garrulus 172
Python amethystinus 221
Python molurus 221, 279
Python reticulatus 221, 279
Python sebae 221, 279
Pyxicephalus adspersus 49

Ramphotyphlops braminus 209
Rana oxyrhyncha 32
Rana sylvatica 254
Rana temporaria 42, 255
Rhacophorus nigropalmatus 32
Rheobatrachus silus 58
Rhinoderma darwini 58
Rhinotyphlops schlegeli 209

Salamandra salamandra 20, 256
Scaphiodontophis annulatus 237
Scincus scincus 196
Siphonops annulatus 28
Sphenondon punctata 271-3, **272**
Stegosaurus 274

Testudo graeca 72
Testudo hermanni 72, 74, **74**
Thamnophis sirtalis parietalis 269
Thecadactylus 172
Thelatornis 225
Tiktaalik 10, **11**
Tiliqua adelaidensis 194
Tiliqua rugosa 190
Tiliqua scincoides 190
Trachemys scripta elegans 94
Trachyboa 207
Triassochelys 69
Trichobatrachus robustus 39
Triturus cristatus 18-20, **19-20**
Tropidophorus 197
Typhlosaurus 197
Tyrannosaurus 275, 277

Uroplatus fimbriatus 177
Uroplatus phantasticus 177
Uta stansburiana 261

Varanus giganteus 187
Varanus varius 189
Velociraptor 277
Vipera berus 266